THE LYNTON & BARNSTAPLE RAILWAY

THE LYNTON & BARNSTAPLE RAILWAY

by

G. A. BROWN

J. D. C. A. PRIDEAUX

H. G. RADCLIFFE

David & Charles
Newton Abbot   London   North Pomfret (Vt)

British Library Cataloguing in Publication Data
Brown, G. A.
 The Lynton & Barnstaple railway.—2nd ed.
 1. Lynton & Barnstaple Railway—History
 I. Title II. Prideaux, J. D. C. A.
 III. Radcliffe, H. G.
 385'.52'0942352   HE3821.L9
 ISBN 0-7153-4958-9

First published 1964
New edition 1971
Second impression 1980
Third impression 1986

© G. A. Brown, J. D. C. A. Prideaux,
H. G. Radcliffe 1964, 1971, 1980

All rights reserved. No part of this
publication may be reproduced, stored
in retrieval system, or transmitted,
in any form or by any means, electronic,
mechanical, photocopying, recording or
otherwise, without the prior permission
of David & Charles Publishers plc

Printed in Great Britain
by Redwood Burn Ltd   Trowbridge   Wilts
for David & Charles Publishers plc
Brunel House   Newton Abbot   Devon

Published in the United States of America
by David & Charles Inc
North Pomfret   Vermont 05053   USA

Contents

    LIST OF ILLUSTRATIONS 9

1 THE FIRST STEPS   11

    The Lynton & Barnstaple · Exmoor transport · rival proposals · the Bill is approved

2 CONSTRUCTION (1895-1898)   17

    1895 · 1896 · 1897 · 1898 · finance and litigation · the cost rises · the financial position 1897 · company v. contractor

3 OPENING AND INDEPENDENT DAYS (1898-1923)   30

    The line is opened · from the opening to 1900 · 1900-1914 · 1914-1923

4 SOUTHERN DAYS (1923-1935)   39

    New ownership · the beginning of the end · first news of the closure

5 CLOSING, SALE AND AFTER   45

    The last train from Lynton · the sale · today

6 THE ROUTE   51

    Barnstaple to Snapper Halt · Snapper Halt to Bratton Fleming · Bratton Fleming to Parracombe Halt · Parracombe to Lynton

7 LOCOMOTIVES   62

    Locomotives used during construction · the Manning Wardle 2—6—2Ts under independent ownership · the Baldwin 2—4—2T *Lyn* · the 2—6—2Ts under the Southern Railway · comparative dimensions

6 CONTENTS

8 ROLLING STOCK   73

    Passenger carriages · goods stock · goods stock list · service vehicles · notes on the goods stock

9 OPERATION OF THE LINE   87

    Timetables · staff · equipment · goods traffic · the pattern of traffic · the operating technique

10 ANECDOTES AND CONCLUSIONS   106

    Tales of the line · conclusions

NOTES   111

APPENDICES   112

    Chronology · locomotive mileage · length of platforms, etc. · dimensions taken from sale catalogue · station drawings · income and expenditure 1898-1922 · Southern National omnibus services between Barnstaple and Lynton

ACKNOWLEDGMENTS & BIBLIOGRAPHY   126

INDEX   129

Illustrations

between pages 16 and 17

1 *Excelsior* on a contractor's train at Pilton Wharf
2 Track laying in the Yeo Valley
3 *Slave* at the site of Woody Bay station
4 Lancey Brook with inspection trolley
5 *Slave* and *Kilmarnock* testing Chelfham viaduct
6 Chelfham from the north-east, 1898

between pages 32 and 33

7 *Yeo* on a works train at Lynton
8 Delivering rolling stock to Pilton yard
9 The reporters' train at Woody Bay
10 Trial train at Collar Bridge

between pages 40 and 41

11 From the transhipment siding at Barnstaple, 1898
12 Awaiting the connection at Barnstaple
13 *Exe* waiting to shunt at Barnstaple
14 *Lyn* arriving at Barnstaple, 1909
15 *Lyn* at the transhipment siding Barnstaple, 1929
16 Lyn on the carriage shed road at Pilton yard, c.1906
17 Trains prepared for the opening of Pilton yard, 11 May 1898
18 A general view of Pilton, 1926
19 Derailment near Snapper, c.1922

between pages 56 and 57

20 The viaduct near Chelfham
21 Winter trains crossing at Chelfham
22 *Taw* climbing through the woods near Chelfham
23 Climbing from Chelfham with the last train
24 Double-headed train at Chumhill, c.1922
25 & 26 Autumn and spring in the Bratton Valley
27 Looking south from Bratton Fleming, 1898
28 Bratton Fleming in Edwardian days

ILLUSTRATIONS

29 *Lew* awaiting departure for Barnstaple at Bratton Fleming, c.1929

between pages 72 and 73

30 Near Bratton Fleming in July 1925
31 South end of Blackmoor, c.1922
32 *Lyn* taking water at Blackmoor
33 *Yeo* near Blackmoor
34 Parracombe Bank
35 Parracombe Halt
36 *Taw* entering Woody Bay, 1935

between pages 88 and 89

37 Caffyns Halt
38 Climbing through Barbrook Woods
39 Running down from Dean Steep
40 and 41 Entering Lynton, 1935
42 *Yeo* at the buffer stops at Lynton, 1935
43 The first through train, Lynton, 19 March 1898
44 Early days at Lynton
45 *Yeo* at Pilton in original livery
46 *Exe* at Blackmoor, 1925
47 *Lew* and wagon 28312 at Woody Bay, 1935

between pages 100 and 101

48 *Lyn* at Pilton following erection
49 *Lyn* in Pilton workshops, 1926
50 *Lyn* with *Yeo* at Pilton, 1935
51 Saloon brake No. 2, 1898
52 3rd No. 2466, 1935
53 3rd brake No. 4108, 1935

between pages 116 and 117

54 Wagon No. 12, 1898
55 Accident casualty—wagon No. 10, 1913
56 Van No. 47044 on Pilton turntable, 1935
57 *Taw* passing Rolle Quay
58 A selection of L & BR tickets

ILLUSTRATIONS

IN TEXT

General Map	24 and 25
Woody Bay station today	29
Bridge 39 devoid of track	44
The company's crest	49
Layout of Barnstaple and Chelfham	50
Layout of Pilton Yard	52
Gradient profile	56
Layout of Bratton and Blackmoor	58
Layout of Woody Bay and Lynton	60
Yeo, Exe and *Taw* as built 1897	64
Lyn as built	66
Lyn as running in 1935	68
Cab details	70
Passenger rolling stock	74
Goods rolling stock	84 and 85
Opening timetable	87
Final working timetable	95
A driver's report of 1901	104
Base for proposed tank, Bratton Fleming	105
Lynton station elevations as built	118
Lynton station plans and sketch track layout, 1898	119
Lynton goods shed, loco shed and ground frame huts	120
Woody Bay and Blackmoor station building plans	121
Blackmoor station elevations	122

CHAPTER 1

The First Steps

THE LYNTON & BARNSTAPLE

The Lynton & Barnstaple Railway was open for only 37 years and has already been closed for 28. But the live interest in it among local people today is indicated by the number of articles and letters about it in the West Country Press—while a generation of railway enthusiasts unborn when nature first began to spread her mantle over the remains of the line is showing an even keener appreciation than that which watched the passage of the last train. The 1 ft 11½ in. gauge Lynton & Barnstaple, crossing the foothills of Exmoor, will always evoke the imagination if not the memory.

For much of its short life it ran at a serious loss and was deserted by people and goods requiring quick transport. Whether or not the Southern Railway should have closed it in 1935, it had certainly outgrown its usefulness as an all-the-year-round passenger and goods line by then. But the sacrifices of capital and time made by the local promoters were not wholly in vain. There was reason enough for Lynton and Lynmouth people to rejoice when the first train steamed in from the outside world. The population and trade of the twin towns rose rapidly, laying the foundation for greater progress in the motor age. The price of coal fell dramatically.

Unlike most of the railways in North Wales of the same or similar gauge, the Lynton & Barnstaple served no especial industry and was dependent on the general traffic of the district. Though the combined population of Lynton and Lynmouth was little over 2,000, even by 1935 coal always figured prominently in the traffic figures. In early days a shipload of coal for the twin towns berthed at Barnstaple's rail-served Rolle Quay several times a year. On these occasions coal trucks were added to almost every train, while at Lynton a special gang was employed to hurry the emptying of the wagons required back at Barnstaple to complete the clearance of the ship. One consequence of the railway's closure in 1935, incidentally, was an increase in the price of fuel at Lynton, which became—as it had been in 1892—the English town farthest away from a railway.

EXMOOR TRANSPORT

Lynmouth grew up as a fishing village, supported chiefly by the herring industry until the herring shoals deserted the coast in the early part of the 19th century. Above it, Lynton existed on its store cattle trade and the oats and rye grown for local use, these being among the few crops which could flourish on Exmoor's indifferent soil. The twin villages drew modest supplies of coal and lime from small coasting vessels which discharged their cargoes on the beach at Lynmouth.

Prior to road improvements in the first half of the 19th century, most people as well as goods travelled by sea. By land, packhorses and riders had the choice of two main outlets. The route along the coast to the east was shorter to Bristol and London, but difficult, and often impassable in winter and in bad weather. The easier graded tracks to Barnstaple were more favoured. The more popular of these lay *via* Lyndiates Lane, across Lynton and Martinhoe Commons and through Parracombe to a lonely inn on the edge of the moor at Westlandpound. The alternative was *via* Ilkerton Ridge and Challacombe Common to this inn. After refreshments here, man and beast proceeded by an indifferent road to Loxhore Cott, where the River Yeo was crossed to Shirwell and Pilton, and so to Barnstaple.

At the turn of the century, when most of Europe was closed by the Napoleonic Wars, Lynton and Lynmouth began their growth as tourist centres, and this growth led to the demand for improved communications with the rest of the country. The first hotel at Lynmouth was built in 1807 by William Litson, the son of the schoolmaster; he also furnished cottages nearby for letting to visitors.

The canal era made no impact on North Devon, but the opening of the Great Western Railway from Paddington to Bristol in 1841 began to affect travel habits, and from the opening of the North Devon Railway in 1854 many visitors on their way to Lynton came by rail as far as Barnstaple. The North Devon Railway, together with the Exeter & Crediton Railway which it joined, ultimately passed into the control of the London & South Western Railway, with through trains from Waterloo *via* Salisbury and Exeter from March 1863.

This spurred on the GWR to sponsor the Devon & Somerset Railway, incorporated on 29 July 1864, and opened in two stages, from Norton Fitzwarren to Wiveliscombe on 8 June 1871, and thence to Barnstaple on 1 November 1873. In the following year, the GWR opened its line to Minehead, and the LSWR its line from Barnstaple to Ilfracombe, by which time Lynton and Lynmouth were framed by rail services on three sides, with the sea to the north. Yet the residents were still some twenty miles from their nearest station.

While these battles were taking place, horse-drawn coach services had started. From 1841 a service linked Bridgwater with Minehead, and in the early 1850s it was extended to Lynmouth during the summer months. To serve the GWR line from Norton Fitzwarren to Minehead, this coach service operated from Williton in 1862, and from Minehead in 1874, and was maintained by the four-horse coaches *Lorna Doone*, *Katerfelto* and *Red Deer*, which took three hours to complete the journey. Although two more horses helped them to ascend Porlock and Countisbury Hills, it was still necessary to ask able-bodied passengers to get out and walk. The coaches ran daily in the summer and weekly in the winter, and the service survived until 1922, when it was replaced by motor buses.

Once it had become a rail junction, the importance of Barnstaple increased rapidly, and by 1860 coach services were radiating from it to Ilfracombe, Combe Martin and Lynton. So Lynton enjoyed connections with Barnstaple and Minehead, and further services were started from Lynton and Lynmouth to Ilfracombe and Dulverton. By 1880, the Lynton to Barnstaple service was operated by the Jones Brothers of Lynton, with three trips a day in the summer, taking 2h. 50m. to complete the journey. The twenty-seater, four-horse coaches *Royal Mail* and *Glen Lyn* were used, supplemented by a three-horse coach *Tantivy*, and a fine stud of 50 horses was maintained. During the winter *Glen Lyn* and a mail cart were sufficient. The Lynton—Ilfracombe run was operated by *Benita* (noted for its fine team of greys), *Tally Ho!* and *The Foresters*.

By 1856 Lynton could offer three hotels, each vying with the others to lure approaching tourists—observed through telescopes— to patronise it, by providing post-boys at the foot of Lynton Hill with an additional horse to assist the patrons' carriage up to their hotel. Other hotels followed, and the wealthy built their own villas. The twin towns flourished, although the pace of development was checked when most other resorts could be reached by railway.

RIVAL PROPOSALS

The clamour for a railway to the twin towns began in the 1850s. After several abortive attempts, a bill was launched in 1879 for a 22-mile line from South Molton to Lynton, with a capital of £72,000; it was quickly dropped. In 1883 the Barnstaple & Lynton Railway Bill, seeking powers for a line *via* Kentisbury, was published; the promoters withdrew because of opposition from the GWR and the LSWR. In the following year, there was an attempt to promote a line from Filleigh, on the GWR's Barnstaple—Taunton line to Lynton, *via* Bratton Fleming and Blackmoor Gate. Initial opposition from the GWR was soon withdrawn, and in 1885 the Lynton Railway Act was passed. It approved a capital of £83,000, but none of this was subscribed, and no construction undertaken on the section authorised from Castle Hill (Filleigh) to Blackmoor Gate.

The promoters succeeded in obtaining further powers during 1886 for the extension to Lynton, and at the same time authority was granted to adopt any gauge not less than 3 ft, or the Lartigue monorail system. If the latter were adopted, it was planned to operate the line by electricity to be generated by a hydro-electric plant on the River Lyn, and there was provision that the company would not be obliged to carry any single article exceeding one ton in weight. A branch from Blackmoor Gate to Combe Martin was approved under an Act of 1887. In 1890 the same promoters secured a new Act, which permitted the abandonment of all but the Lynton—Blackmoor section, and gave until 1894 to complete the line.

A fresh attempt was made in 1892, by the promotion of a bill to sanction the building of a standard-gauge tramway, from the line already authorised under the 1890 Lynton Act at Blackmoor Gate, to a junction with the LSWR at Braunton, and thence by means of running powers over the LSWR to Barnstaple, changing the name of the whole scheme to 'The Barnstaple and Lynton Electric Tramroad Company'. No doubt the promoters had been watching electric railway developments at Brighton and London when they made this move. Early opposition from the LSWR and several landlords was soon overcome, and the bill passed the House of Lords, but certain amendments were needed to conform with Board of Trade requirements for level crossings, and before these could be incorporated Parliament was dissolved in June 1892. The bill was not proceeded with in the next session, and the powers lapsed.

During the 1880s, Mr and Mrs George Newnes were touring the district in their own carriage and stayed with Mr Thomas Hewitt. They quickly came under the spell of Lynton and Lynmouth, returning each August until in 1892 they built Hollerday House where they spent August, September and Christmas each year, finally retiring there a few years before Sir George died. Sir George, the son of a Congregational minister, made his name as the publisher of such well-known periodicals as *Tit-Bits*, *The Pall Mall Gazette* and the *Strand Magazine*. He entered Parliament as Liberal M.P. for Newmarket in 1885, and received his baronetcy in 1896. He took a lively part in local affairs, making a gift to Lynton of its Town Hall to mark the inception of the Urban District Council in 1894, and together with Mr (later Sir Thomas) Hewitt, K.C., financed the construction of the funicular cliff railway between Lynton and Lynmouth, which was opened in 1890. He also sponsored the building of a hydro-electric plant on the East Lyn River, also opened in 1890, making the twin towns among the first to be lit by electricity.

The success of Spooner's ingenuity on the Festiniog Railway (of 1 ft 11½ in. gauge) and elsewhere so impressed several of Lynton's leading citizens that they felt that something similar might solve the town's problem. Sir George Newnes, together with his friend Mr Hewitt, Mr E. B. Jeune (whose wife was Lady of the Manor), and Mr W. H. Halliday, organised during the summer of 1894 a number of meetings at which the principles adopted by Spooner on the Festiniog Railway were advocated. It was claimed that sharper curves would enable major engineering works to be kept to a minimum, that it would cost only £2,500 per mile compared with £8,000 for standard gauge, and that it would interfere less with the scenery.

Almost at once Lord Fortescue and others promoted an alternative standard-gauge line, which they proposed should run from a junction with the GWR at Filleigh by way of High Bray, Bratton Fleming, Parracombe and Martinhoe Cross to Lynton. They claimed that this was a shorter route than the earlier Filleigh scheme, following high ground rather than the valleys. There would be no major engineering works. Trains would split at Filleigh, the fore part proceeding to Taunton, and the rear part reversing to Barnstaple. This scheme was supported strongly by the GWR and by some local residents, but the influence of Sir George Newnes and his colleagues in favour of the narrow-gauge line to Barnstaple was undoubtedly stronger.

THE BILL IS APPROVED

On 19 March 1895 the committee of the House of Lords considered the two schemes, and after eight days it approved the Lynton & Barnstaple bill and rejected the Filleigh scheme. A petition prepared against the bill was later withdrawn. Meanwhile, local support for it was increasing. In May, a public meeting at Lynton enthusiastically backed a petition in support of the bill then before Parliament. The Chairman, Mr J. Heywood, emphasised that the line took them where they wanted to go, that it was an honest scheme, and that the sponsors had a local interest, as property owners, in the progress of Lynton. There seems little doubt that the last reason played a great part in influencing local opinion to support the bill.

Critics of the change of gauge at Barnstaple were met by the statement that water-borne goods, in particular coal, would be landed direct into the company's wagons at the quay in Barnstaple. Much more coal, lime and other merchandise was of course carried by sea into North Devon in those days than after the first world war. An exchange station was planned with the LSWR Ilfracombe line at Barnstaple, complete with facilities for transhipping goods. This was eventually built as Barnstaple Town, replacing an existing LSWR station, Barnstaple Quay, sited slightly nearer the Junction. To increase confidence in the scheme, Sir George Newnes stated that standard-gauge wagons might be run on to the narrow-gauge ones, to eliminate transhipment, but nothing further was heard of this idea.

Finally all opposition was withdrawn, and on 27 June 1895 the bill received Royal Assent. It authorised a capital of £72,000 and borrowing powers of £23,300. The registered offices were at the premises of the company's bankers, Messrs Fox, Fowler & Co., Church Street, Lynton, with Mr F. B. Erridge as secretary. Mr C. E. Roberts Chanter of Barnstaple was appointed solicitor, and Sir James Szlumper consulting engineer.

Everything was set for a start to be made on the Lynton & Barnstaple Railway.

CONSTRUCTION
(1) *'Excelsior'* on a contractor's train at Pilton Wharf
(2) *Track laying in the Yeo Valley*
(3) *'Slave'* at the site of Woody Bay station

THE VIADUCTS

(4) *Lancey Brook—with inspection trolley*
(5) *'Slave' and 'Kilmarnock' testing Chelfham viaduct*
(6) *Chelfham from the north-east 1898*

Chapter 2

Construction 1895-1898

1895

The first meeting of the board of the new company was held on 28 June 1895, the day after the bill received the Royal Assent. Sir George Newnes was appointed chairman, with Messrs E. B. Jeune, T. Hewitt and W. H. Halliday as directors, and Mr Francis William Chanter (brother of the company's solicitor) was instructed to lay out the line of the railway and prepare all necessary plans. The route from Barnstaple was to follow the River Yeo for five miles or so before climbing the slopes of Bratton Down to the fringe of Exmoor at Blackmoor Gate, whence it crossed the valley of the River Heddon on an embankment at Parracombe, and then proceeded *via* Martinhoe Cross and the valley of the West Lyn River to a terminus at Shambleway, near Lynbridge.

In August, Lady Newnes was asked to 'honour the directors by cutting the first sod', which she did at the site of Lynton station on 17 September. The promoters' optimism was evident from the shortened prospectus and advertisements, issued on 2 November, which estimated that a considerable excursion traffic would be attracted to the line, citing in support the fact that over thirty four-horse brakes a day entered Lynton in the season. To capture this traffic, much of which came from Ilfracombe, passengers would be encouraged to transfer from coach to train at Blackmoor, therefore saving time on their journey and sparing the horses the more difficult part of the route. The station at Martinhoe Cross, called 'Wooda Bay', was intended to serve Woody Bay, three miles away, which was being developed by a syndicate as a rival resort to Lynmouth. Land for the station was donated to the company and it was the intention eventually to build a branch to Woody Bay, but the syndicate soon used up its financial resources, and Woody Bay did not flourish. Further misplaced optimism was shown in the expected journey time from Barnstaple to Lynton of one hour, which also failed to materialise.

The company's first ordinary meeting took place on 17 December 1895, with Mr Jeune in the chair. All directors were re-elected. About this time it was decided that solicitors, engineers, surveyor and secretary should all submit weekly reports, which would go first to Mr Hewitt.

1896

In March 1896 the solicitors were told to obtain possession of the necessary land, and the engineer to complete plans for Barnstaple Town station which would require the approval of Barnstaple Corporation as alterations at the mouth of the River Yeo were involved. In April it was decided that a siding and stopping place should be provided at Hunnacott, between Bratton and Blackmoor. The engineer advertised for two clerks of works to superintend construction at salaries of £2 10s and £2 2s weekly, and was instructed to report on the question of water supply at Blackmoor Gate. In less conventional vein, it was minuted 'that provision be made in the fencing for the passage of deer at certain places to be arranged with Mr Jeune'. A further reference to this appeared in a 1917 guide book: 'Soon after leaving Bratton, the line runs in a perfect horseshoe which practically closes the Bratton Valley. The opening made in the bank, spanned by a bridge, was made in order to give wild deer a chance to escape when pursued by huntsmen.'

In May, the proposed sites for Bratton and Chelfham stations were approved and it was decided that in view of landowners' opposition the proposed siding at Hunnacott would have to be abandoned. Sir George Newnes wrote to the LSWR's solicitors, pointing out the inconvenience being caused to the company and the contractor by the delay in reaching agreement on various points. The engineer presented a very lucid report on the approach road to Lynton station. Four routes were possible, but one could be ruled out through opposition from the landowner. The engineer favoured two of the others, with particular preference for that past Dykes Cottage which permitted an easier gradient. This route was approved by Lynton Council, to be constructed at a cost of not more than £800.

As deadlock still existed with the LSWR in July, the board re solved to build an independent station at Barnstaple. The threat had its effect, and on 17 August 1896 a revised agreement was approved. Four days later, after considerable discussion, Mr F. W. Chanter (the engineer) was instructed to obtain specifications, plans and tenders for the construction of the type of locomotive he thought would best meet the company's needs. In November a proposed deviation at Martinhoe Cross was considered, and it was left for Mr Jeune and Mr Hewitt to see a local landowner with a view to siting the station nearer Parracombe.

1897

In seconding the directors' report in February, Mr Jeune stated that on the previous day he had travelled over Chelfham viaduct with 110 men and 28 trucks of earth and there had not been the slightest sign of deflection. He produced photographs of the train and viaduct and said that the line from Barnstaple to Chelfham had actually been laid, and that shortly it would be possible to run the 12½ miles to Bratton.[1] By the end of March the line as far as Parracombe would be ready, and all the large works would be completed by the middle of April. The contractor had promised that he would have men working night and day in order to obtain a Board of Trade inspection by about 12 June. At the same meeting, a memorial from Parracombe to alter the position of Martinhoe station was refused, as it was now too late for changes.

In July the board had to consider what to do with the locomotives and rolling stock until the line was completed. The water supply was giving concern, and Mr Jeune was asked to negotiate lowest terms with the Lynton Water Company. The engineer was asked to report on the position at other stations. Mr Nuttall[2] was claiming his right to construct the stations, but the board declined to recognise it, and had in fact already made arrangements with Jones Brothers of Lynton. Purchase of two inspection trolleys, the turntable, and the hot air engines (for the stations) was approved.

During August, the goods wagons were ordered and fares fixed at 1d per mile third class and 2½d per mile first class, with first return at single fare plus a half. Tenders were accepted for the supply of water at Barnstaple, Chelfham, Bratton and Blackmoor; the refreshment rooms were put out to tender; certain works at the station yard at Barnstaple were approved.

The eighteenth of October was a noteworthy date, for on this day the board had Sir James Szlumper and Mr Nuttall junr. both in attendance. In reply to the chairman, Sir James assured them that his only connection with Mr Nuttall was as engineer of a line in Wales on which Mr Nuttall was engaged—its name was not revealed—and that no undue favour was being extended to him.

'Junior' was then put on the carpet and in reply to the chairman's charge of want of energy and request for evidence of progress, he assured them that every exertion was being made to complete the line. He promised—as the minute book records, 'most faithfully'—that the line would be open to goods traffic by 1 January. It will be recalled that in February 1897 the contractor had sought an extension until 1 July; yet in October his son was promising completion by 1 January 1898. It is not hard to imagine the anxiety which every member of the board must have felt at this continual delay. At the conclusion of these interviews, which must have been held in a rather strained atmosphere, Sir James Szlumper agreed to write to the contractor. After this, the board went on to consider the application from Mr McDougall of the North Wales Narrow Gauge Railway for the post of accountant, and to agree with Mr Chanter that his own salary (as general manager) should commence three months before the line opened. It also approved pits he had asked for, presumably in the loco shed. In November the problem of providing water at Lynton, in view of the high cost of obtaining it from the Lynton Water Company, was discussed, and Mr R. Pilkington was selected as the first engine driver, to start work from delivery of the first locomotive.

1898

Early in January 1898 the question of metalling the platforms and approaches to the stations was tackled, together with the decision to appoint a permanent way inspector. The following month it was decided to obtain a fourth engine from Manning, Wardle & Co. or elsewhere, provided it could be available by 1 July. Mr R. Fursden was appointed stationmaster at Lynton 'at 25s per week with quarters, coal, light, uniform of a coat, waistcoat, cap and two pairs of trousers per annum, with fourteen days' notice on either side to determine within which period possession of the quarters to be given'. Under somewhat similar terms Thomas Dewfall was appointed station master at Bratton at 21s a week, and the executive committee were left to appoint 'as they think best' at the other stations. It was also decided that the opening ceremony should be on 29 April, the public opening following a few days later. A draft timetable was considered, and Mr McDougall appointed traffic manager and accountant at £125 per annum. Mr Jeune was asked to negotiate with Ilfracombe coach proprietors for through booking arrangements, and Mr Bentley's tender for 200 tons of coal at 16s per ton, to be delivered in 50-ton lots as required, was accepted.

The first train, consisting of *Taw* and one coach, ran through to Lynton on Monday 14 March 1898, and two days later, on the invitation of Mr F. W. Chanter, a party of Press representatives and officials left Pilton yard at about 10.15 a.m. in a composite coach with a first saloon at the rear, behind *Yeo*, with driver Pilkington and fireman Willis. The journey took 1h. 35m., excluding stops, and at Lynton the party were entertained to lunch at the Manor House by Mr Jeune. The return journey took ten minutes less. They were able to see for themselves the high standard of the civil engineering works.

Early in April 1898 it was agreed to build station masters' cottages at Bratton and Chelfham at a cost not exceeding £200; in practice the company's finances never allowed this to be done. Messrs Sanders & Co. and Messrs Evans, O'Donnell & Co. were invited to quote for the maintenance of signalling and telegraph apparatus, while Jones Brothers were told to lay water pipes from Dean to Lynton. The manager was given instructions to make the best terms he could with Messrs W. H. Smith & Son regarding bookstalls, and arrangements were made for the official opening of the line. The board fixed the date for 11 May; Sir George and Lady Newnes were 'invited and requested to take upon themselves the opening ceremony' which it was decided should take place at Barnstaple. After this the first train would leave at 11.15 a.m., arriving at Lynton at 12.45 p.m., with the second train following 15 minutes later, and lunch would be served at the Valley of Rocks Hotel, Lynton, at 1.30 p.m. It was also agreed that invitations should be limited to 150, and finally that Sir George should consult with the engineer about the purchase of the new engine from Baldwins of Philadelphia and order it.

The official Board of Trade inspection took place early in May. Lasting for nine hours, it included testing each bridge with two locomotives, and proved satisfactory to Colonel Yorke, the inspecting officer. A private celebration made by the company before the official opening ended rather ignominiously at Wooda Bay, where the locomotive, which was hauling four coaches, failed through overloading, and the party had to continue to the Valley of Rocks Hotel, where they were to be entertained, in horse-drawn carriages!

The line was finally opened on 11 May 1898, and on that day Mr Halliday died. Perhaps at this point it is well to reflect on the intolerable burden shouldered by these founder directors during the trying period from the launching of the line until it was finally opened. All of them were public figures in the area, with other business interests, yet for the small fee of £50 per annum each they had devoted an enormous amount of time and effort to reaching a successful conclusion to their plans. For this reason, and because of the interesting decisions they were called upon to make, there has been no hesitation in quoting freely from the company's minute book. Unfortunately, fewer details of the later years are available, but at least it has been possible to give full details of each step from a time when the line was just a pipe-dream until it became an actual working reality.

FINANCE AND LITIGATION

Although the railway was eventually opened with some success, there had been a rather painful financial background, which culminated in legal proceedings between contractor and company.

The financial story began in June 1895 when £500 was deposited with the Postmaster General in accordance with Clause 43 of the Lynton & Barnstaple Railway Act. By early July the company had entered into correspondence with the LSWR and GWR regarding rebates and interchange facilities, and a month later, with plans well in hand, the bankers were asked for an overdraft of £1,000. In October the directors appointed Mr F. W. Chanter as engineer for £2,000, to cover fees and expenses from the passing of the Act to the final completion of the line (including Board of Trade certificate) and the cost of at least one assistant. At the same time payments of £300 for expenses prior to the passing of the Act were paid to Messrs F. W. Chanter, Smith Richards, and Jones Brothers.

In November the secretary's salary was fixed at £100 per annum, to include provision of an office, and at the same time a committee of the entire board was formed to attend to land purchase.

In March 1896 the first real steps were taken, when the board announced that it had accepted the tender of £42,100 from Mr James Nuttall of Moss Side, Manchester, to build the line, and had agreed to add another £500 for completion by 1 May 1897. This came as a surprise locally, as it had generally been supposed that Jones Brothers would secure the contract, particularly as one of the partners had surveyed the route to Blackmoor, but their tender was considerably higher at £48,000. In April a call was made for £2 per share to be paid by 1 May. Shareholders were advised that the contract had been made with Mr Nuttall, who had begun work and was under agreement to complete the line by 1 May 1897.

THE COST RISES

In May 1896, large amounts in excess of estimates were being claimed and paid for land. This was drawn to the surveyor's attention and he was asked to consider whether any steps could be taken to obtain a reduction on the grounds of severance.

The second half-yearly meeting was held on 5 September, when only five people attended, including two directors. A further call of £2 a share was made a week later. On 22 September, Mr R. Jones attended a board meeting and was asked to give plans and estimates for stations, and a week later the draft agreement with the LSWR was finally approved for 30 years, by which the company paid £150 per annum, £140 for the use of Barnstaple Town station, and terminal charges not exceeding £10. But the solicitors were empowered to agree £160 per annum to include terminal charges on parcels, mails and dogs, where these were not interchanged in traffic not exceeding £10.

In November, the lowest tender for locomotives was accepted, which was that from Manning, Wardle & Company at £1,100 each, together with a tender of £7,300 from the Bristol Wagon Company Ltd. for 16 carriages. This latter contract carried a ten per cent discount, presumably for prompt payment. The final call of £2 a share was made in December, and the question of raising a debenture loan was discussed. Application to the Board of Trade for a provisional order to raise a further £15,000 was confirmed.

In moving the adoption of the directors' report at the third half-yearly meeting on 24 February 1897, the chairman stated that the contractor had asked for an extension until 1 July and for the penalty clause to be waived, both of which requests the board had refused. He was glad to be able to report that the contracts for locomotives, rolling stock, signalling and telegraph equipment had been placed at less than the original estimates, but land had cost three times more than expected, and in view of possible increased traffic in the future, the directors had deemed it prudent to buy enough land to permit the line to be doubled throughout if necessary. The report was carried unanimously, and the directors authorised to raise £23,300 debentures, as provided for in the Act. At a special board meeting the same day, the creation of £15,000 new stock was authorised.

By this time the board was facing great difficulties. Less than two years before, on the authority of the consulting engineer, it was

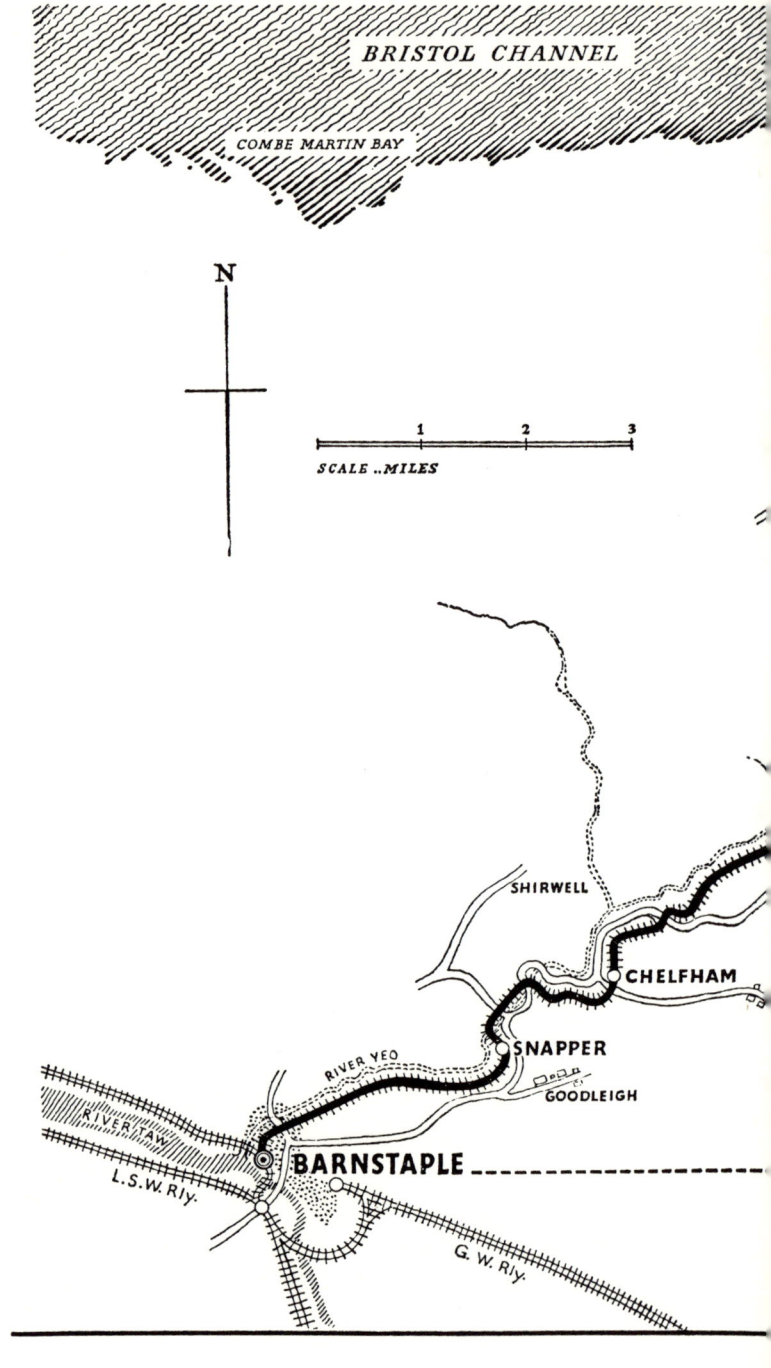

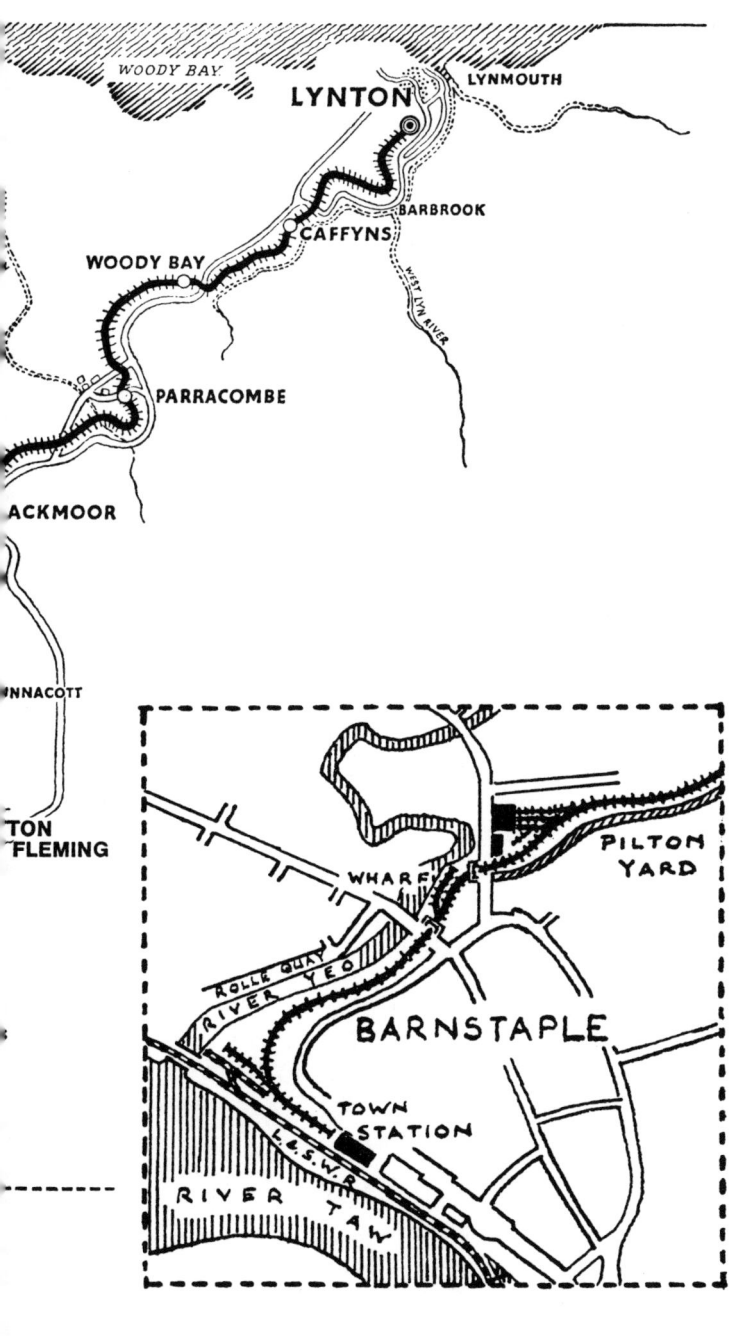

stated in the prospectus that the line could be built for a sum not exceeding £50,000, that it would contain no major engineering works, and would be open to traffic by the summer of 1897, completed and equipped without recourse to the company's borrowing powers. The consulting engineer misled not only the company, but the contractor as well, for the latter found that, far from having a 'surface line' to construct, he was in fact involved in a vast amount of earthworks, much of the excavation being in rock and costing him £22,000 more than he had allowed for in his tender. Unusually wet weather had delayed the work, and particularly the settling of earthworks took longer. In February 1897, about two months before the estimated opening date, with its funds all but exhausted, the board was thus having to raise extra capital in order to continue, and with only a vague promise that the line would be open by mid-June. It had budgeted for being able to carry some holiday traffic in 1897, and so start off with a period of good operating receipts, which with reasonable fortune should have carried the company through the lean months of its first winter. The founder-directors, these four stout-hearted citizens of Lynton, could not possibly, in their wildest moments, have known the burden they were to shoulder, when they accepted their directorships in the company. The twenty-fourth of February must have been one of the board's hardest days, for after the half-yearly meeting and special meeting to create the additional stock, the four worthies ploughed into a board meeting where they started by approving the purchase of roller bearings for the coaches at a cost of £500 less 10 per cent, and the supply of signalling and telegraph equipment by Messrs Evans, O'Donnell & Co. Ltd. for £2,025. The chairman's attitude towards the contractors' requests was supported.

At the same meeting Mr Frank W. Chanter was appointed manager of the railway at a salary of £250 per annum, to start from 1 May. This arrangement did not interfere with his post as engineer. The position did not improve, and in July a loan was being arranged for £16,000 with the company's bankers, Fox, Fowler & Co., at 4 per cent, the security being the company's mortgage debentures for £21,996 13s 4d.

THE FINANCIAL POSITION 1897

During August, a further £15,000 ordinary shares and £5,000 debentures were created. At this stage, it is convenient to recall the financial position. £72,000 ordinary shares were provided for under the Act, £15,000 more created on 24 February 1897, and this further £15,000 on 28 August 1897. In addition, £23,300 debentures were raised on 24 February, plus a further £5,000 on 28 August. Thus some £20,000 had been put into the company over and above the original estimate, yet the line was still incomplete.

Some action had obviously to be taken, yet the first step was a letter from the secretary to Sir James Szlumper (the consulting engineer) calling attention to the gross breach of contract which existed. During September, four spare axle boxes for the coaches were ordered, and an estimate of £144 10s 0d from Messrs Sanders & Ridges for the goods shed at Barnstaple was accepted.

About the time of the meeting in October 1897, when the contractor was promising completion by 1 January 1898, the board's anxiety at the increasing financial burden which the company would have to shoulder before a single ticket could be issued was increased by reports that Mr Nuttall was in financial difficulties, and although this was absolutely denied by his son, the report proved to be the shadow of forthcoming events.

The first call of £2 on the new shares was also made in November, when estimates were sought for stabling at Blackmoor Gate for 20 horses, and tenders for 100 tons of coal a month for three months were put out. The second call on the shares was made early in January 1898 and the third in April 1898.

COMPANY V. CONTRACTOR

Although it took place after the opening, it is appropriate to deal here with the legal battle between the company and the contractor. The contractor claimed an extra £40,000. The company repudiated this and began an action against Mr Nuttall to obtain an order that the contract was still in force and uncancelled. In August 1898 the company was arranging legal representation at the arbitration. Subsequently, the arbitrator, Sir James Szlumper, awarded £27,000 to Mr Nuttall for blasting and extra work, and in December, Messrs Mellor, Smith & May were retained to act with Messrs Finch & Chanter, the company's solicitors, to prepare their case for the Divisional Court against Mr Nuttall and the arbitration award, the board paying the two firms £300 and £250 respectively. On 20 February 1899 the board heard that the Divisional Court decision on the arbitration appeal was in favour of the company on all points, with costs. It had then to consider the item of £2,317 awarded by the Court to Mr Nuttall beyond the items appealed against, and the best way of raising money to pay off this sum and one of £1,166 admittedly due to the contractor. In March, it was learnt that Mr Nuttall had appealed against the Divisional Court's decision. The outcome of the appeal can best be given by quoting the *North Devon Herald*:

> There can be no doubt that the decision of the Appeal Court in *re* Nuttall v. Lynton & Barnstaple Railway Company is a just one, and however hard the result may be upon the plaintiff, who was the contractor, the Company has won fairly and squarely all through the litigation. Five judges have now given it as their opinion—two in the Divisional and three in the Appeal Court—and Sir James Szlumper, the arbitrator, was altogether wrong in awarding a sum of money to Mr Nuttall, because he had to do some extra and unexpected work in building the line. It was Mr Nuttall's business to find out beforehand what he had to do, and then to make his charges for doing it. Instead of this, however, the contractor bound himself by a solemn agreement to carry out the contract for better or worse—unfortunately for him it proved to be worse. Having to his astonishment to excavate rock instead of clay, he sought to go behind a special clause in the agreement which explicitly stated that there were to be no 'extras', and demanded an extra payment of about £27,000, which the arbitrator, Sir James Szlumper, promptly awarded him. The reversal of this award by the Divisional Court, and the confirmation of such reversal by the Appeal Court, may possibly open up the all-important question of arbitration, and throw a slur upon it which it certainly does not deserve; this, of course, would be most regrettable, but, so far as the question of the Lynton & Barnstaple Railway Company's position is concerned, there cannot be two opinions as to the justice of the decision arrived at. Let us hope that the decision will be accepted as absolutely final, for nothing would be gained by a further appeal.

It is a matter of some amazement that the amount of Mr Nuttall's claim almost doubled his original tender, and even the figure awarded by the arbitrator added more than 50 per cent to the tender. One is left to assume that the specifications and quantities (if these were issued) for the purpose of tender were inaccurate and misleading, or that the contractor had failed to acquaint himself with the nature and scope of the work before preparing his estimates.

By the time the Appeal Court's decision was known, Mr Nuttall had gone bankrupt, so the company was unable to reap any financial benefit from the decision, and moreover had to bear its own heavy legal expenses. Just as important, it lost the benefit of a clause in the original contract with Mr Nuttall, whereby he undertook to maintain the track for a year after completion.

In May 1899 the board decided to close its account with Messrs

Fox, Fowler & Co. and to open one with the National Provincial Bank, Barnstaple, in order to raise the amount needed to meet its liability to the contractor. As the company's secretary, Mr Erridge, was also the manager of Fox, Fowler & Co., the board regretfully decided to dismiss him.

Undoubtedly much of the blame for the company's unsatisfactory financial position must fall upon the consulting engineer. His early comments showed little appreciation of the task involved in construction. Some of the specifications seem ill-suited, and in particular the choice of a minimum radius of five chains for the curvature of a 2 ft gauge line in difficult country was extremely generous, where sharper curves might have avoided some expensive earthworks. Unfortunately other factors combined to limit operating speeds and the company was thus prevented from turning this expensive asset to advantage. The consulting engineer had forecast the overall journey time as an hour: in practice this was never reduced below 90 minutes.

Woody Bay station today

CHAPTER 3

Opening and Independent Days 1898-1923

THE LINE IS OPENED

Instructions for the opening have come down to us from some detailed notes left by the late Mr F. E. Box, and they are worthy of quoting in full, though photographs suggest that they may not have been strictly adhered to.

At 11 a.m. a light engine (Driver Milne, Fireman Pine) will leave the yard and run through to Lynton where they will shunt on to the engine house siding. At 11.15 a.m. it will leave Barnstaple Town Station for Lynton as follows:

Barnstaple Town	dep. 11.15 a.m.	Driver Lodge
Barnstaple Yard	pass 11.18 ,,	Fireman Glover
Chelfham	pass 11.40 ,,	Guard Glover
Bratton	arr. 11.55 ,,	Carriages 6, 4 and 2
	Water if necessary	
	dep. 12.5 p.m.	
Blackmoor	pass 12.25 p.m.	
Wooda Bay	pass 12.44 ,,	
Lynton	arr. 1.00 ,,	

On arrival at Lynton, engine will halt short of ribbon, and then advance to end of platform when same is cut. The engine and train will remain at Platform No. 1 until after the arrival of the second train. Both will probably have to go to Wooda Bay for water. The second train will leave Barnstaple Town at 11.40 p.m. as per following timetable:

Barnstaple Town	dep. 11.40 a.m.	Driver Pilkington
Barnstaple Yard	pass 11.43 ,,	Fireman Willis
Chelfham	pass 12.1 p.m.	Guard Pargeter
Bratton	pass 12.25 ,,	Carriages 5, 3 and 1
Blackmoor	pass 12.45 ,,	
Wooda Bay	pass 1.05 ,,	
Lynton	arr. 1.20 ,,	

This train will run into Bay at Lynton. As soon as platforms are clear of passengers, the train must be shunted ready for the return journeys with carriages No. 1 and No. 2 at rear, and on returning Driver Pilkington will start first with train Driver Lodge took up. First return train:

Lynton	dep. 5.20 p.m.
Wooda Bay	pass 5.37 „
Blackmoor	pass 6.00 „
Bratton	pass 6.22 „
Chelfham	pass 6.37 „
Barnstaple Yard	pass 6.57 „
Barnstaple Town	arr. 7.00 „

Driver to run round train and take it to yard. Signalman Masters to note that second train must not leave Chelfham until first train is safe in yard.

Driver Lodge will leave Lynton with the train that arrived second at 5.45 p.m. and will run as per the following times:

Lynton	dep. 5.45 p.m.
Wooda Bay	pass 6.01 „
Blackmoor	pass 6.22 „
Bratton	pass 6.46 „
Chelfham	pass 7.06 „
Barnstaple Town	arr. 7.27 „

All carriages required must be taken by the engine two at a time by 9 a.m. in the following order—Yard 6, 4, 2, 5, 3, 1—Town Station, so that the second engine can go back to Town Station light and stand in Dock Road until first train has gone away, and then back on to 5, 3, 1 ready to start.

All signals necessary must be worked by Stationmaster. Gateman Bray to be on duty at Braunton Road, and Signalman Masters at Pilton Bridge Box.

Foreman Fitter Pearce to see that all coaches are well oiled and doors of carriages locked.

These plans and all the other arrangements having been made, the line was duly opened on Wednesday 11 May 1898. Barnstaple Corporation procession assembled at the Guildhall and left at 10.45 a.m. to be met on the steps of Barnstaple Town station by Sir George Newnes, Lady Newnes, Frank Newnes, Sir Cameron Gull, Mr Vallance, and Mr Jacomb Hood of the LSWR and Mr F. W. Chanter, engineer of the L & BR.

In performing the opening ceremony at the station, Sir George said they were allowing 1h. 40m. because the track was new. They wanted a punctual line and hoped and intended that the time would be reduced to one hour. The first train was hauled by *Yeo*, and subsequently commemorative medals were presented to all elementary schoolchildren. A triumphal arch greeted it at Bratton, where the Parish Council presented an address to Sir George. Stops occupied 26 mins and the first train arrived at 1.17 p.m. at Lynton, where it stopped just short of the station to allow Lady Newnes to alight and perform the opening by cutting the red, white and blue ribbons which were extended across the track.

In his address at Lynton station, Sir George said that no doubt some wished the line had taken them a little closer to the town, but there were engineering difficulties, besides which they were anxious that the railway should not in any way disfigure their beautiful little Alpine villages.

The scene at Lynton station was one of great festivity and excitement, with the lifeboatmen in full kit festooned on the signal posts to obtain a better view. When the second train arrived, the party proceeded to the Valley of Rocks Hotel, where the company entertained the mayor and corporation of Barnstaple and Lynton Urban Council and others to lunch. In the course of his reply to the toast of the company, Sir George stated that the cost of the land had been enormous, five times its real value according to one authority. 'It is nothing but downright robbery,' said Sir George. He also referred to a proposal for a line from Minehead *via* Countisbury to Lynmouth, which he hoped would not come to anything, as it would be detrimental to the beauty of the countryside.

The line was opened to general traffic on the following Monday 16 May, the first train for Lynton leaving at 8.49 a.m. (presumably the 8.46 a little late). A report in the *North Devon Journal* on 19 May records that both this train and the next one 'conveyed a good complement of passengers to Lynton, and the trains running to Barnstaple were equally well patronised'. Hotel omnibuses met the trains at Lynton, and about 1,200 passengers a week were carried during May. The last horse-drawn coach service was also run, and outside the coach station in Joy Street were the words 'Farewell ye Coaches' and 'Success to the Lynton & Barnstaple Railway'. Mr Baker, the coach driver, became station master at Chelfham, and survived to witness the last train pass through Bratton Fleming station thirty-seven years later.

FROM THE OPENING TO 1900

The first board meeting after the opening was held on 30 June. It was agreed to meet a request from the inhabitants of Bratton Fleming to change the name of their station from Bratton to Bratton Fleming. A request from the engine drivers for more pay was not however considered so favourably! Presumably the original drivers were never satisfied on this point, for by 1901 they appear to have left the employ of the company, records showing the three

PREPARING THE LINE FOR TRAFFIC—1
(7) *'Yeo' on a works train at Lynton*
(8) *Delivering rolling stock to Pilton yard*
(9) *The reporters' train at Woody Bay*

OPENING AND INDEPENDENT DAYS 1898—1923

drivers on duty on 5 and 6 September of that year to be H. Fennell, W. T. Willis and F. Northcombe. The board also heard the developments in the action with Mr Nuttall. By August the line was carrying 2,100 passengers a week, and on the 5th the directors decided to lower the first class fare from Barnstaple to Lynton from 4s 2d to 3s, and the return fare from 6s 3d to 5s. Third class fares for the same journey remained at 1s 7½d single, 3s 3d return, dogs 6d (any distance), and cycles 1s (any distance).

Lyn, which had been built by Baldwins in May 1898, arrived and was assembled, and after modification entered service; it melted a fusible plug on its first run.

During their August meeting the board dealt with improvements to the approach roads at Wooda Bay, Blackmoor, and Bratton Fleming stations, and the provision of crossings at stations between the up and down platforms. They also decided to retain counsel for opposing the Minehead & Lynmouth Railway Scheme, and also the arbitration of the contractor's claim for £40,000 (not £27,000 as stated by the *North Devon Herald* in their report after the Appeal Court's decision), which they had repudiated; they wished to postpone the arbitration to enable more evidence to be obtained and to see whether Sir Douglas Fox would give evidence on their behalf.

The Minehead & Lynmouth Light Railway was planned to be 2 ft gauge, and to start alongside the GWR station at Minehead, run to Porlock, then follow the coastline along to a terminus at the Tors at Lynmouth. The total distance was just over 20 miles, the maximum gradient 1 in 40, and the sharpest curve 60 ft radius. A proposed branch to Minehead pier was dropped through local opposition. A public enquiry held by the Light Railway Commissioners at Minehead resulted in the whole plan being dropped because of strong opposition from Lynton and Lynmouth. Sir George Newnes gave evidence that the opening of the Lynton & Barnstaple Railway rendered the proposed line unnecessary, but as it was intended purely for tourist traffic, it might well have succeeded where the L & BR failed.

At the company's sixth half-yearly meeting on 24 September the Rev J. Chanter asked about Parracombe station, and was told that the Board of Trade inspector had sanctioned the stopping of trains on Fridays to take up or set down, and that the directors would be considering stopping trains there shortly. A month later the directors decided to apply for membership of the Railway Clearing House, and the manager was instructed to obtain tenders for two supplies of coal of 60 tons each from the pithead, unloading to be undertaken by the company. In view of the financial situation, Mr Jeune's offer to provide the company with a workshop at 4 per cent interest on the capital outlay was also gratefully accepted.

In the year 1899 the litigation with Mr Nuttall the contractor, described in the last chapter, gave the board some anxious sessions. Early in the year Mr Chanter resigned as general manager, and at the March meeting the board appointed Mr Charles E. Drewett temporarily to the post of traffic manager for six months from 1 May following, at a salary of £200 per annum, the LSWR being asked to give him leave of absence. In the same month Mr Jeune was appointed 'local director with power of a committee to supervise details of management' and between them, he and Mr Drewett, who was appointed secretary and general manager later on in November, ran the railway for the remainder of its independent existence.

By August, the financial arrangements for carrying mails were well in hand and Mr Hewitt reported that he had made a claim for £300 per annum as from 16 May 1898. At the same meeting Mr Jeune recommended that a new shed be erected at Barnstaple at a cost of about £100. This was the additional carriage road between the engine shed and the main carriage shed, which was not covered when the line was opened. Just a month earlier, Parracombe had featured for the first time in public timetables as a regular halt. While only the Friday market trains stopped here, it had been the duty of the Blackmoor porter to issue tickets. But as the halt's service increased, tickets were issued from the village post office—an unusual practice which continued for many years. Parracombe water was excellent for locomotive purposes and a supply was laid on during the first few years.

By this time the South African War was in progress, and Fireman Willis had been recalled as a reservist. At the November meeting the board agreed to pay his wife 5s a week during his absence. At the same meeting the board, as an economy measure, examined the possibility of running two trains a day instead of three during winter months. Requests for a shelter at Parracombe, and a footpath from the down platform at Chelfham to the main road, to shorten the route to Loxhore, were met by the board at about this time.

1900 TO 1914

Some relics of the contractor's days still lay around, and early in the new century locomotive *Kilmarnock* was sold, and a six-ton

OPENING AND INDEPENDENT DAYS 1898—1923

coal truck, No. 19, was added to the stock. It is believed that this was also part of the contractor's *débris*. During the year, Mr Henry Sowden, stationmaster at Blackmoor, left to become general manager of the Bideford, Westward Ho! & Appledore Railway. Coal prices had risen, for in 1900 a contract was made with a company in the Powell Group to supply 600 tons at 24s 4d a ton.

In February 1903, the weather was very severe and snow made the line impassable for several days. A gang of a dozen men dug out some of the cuttings where snow ten feet deep had drifted. In the same year an eight-ton open bogie wagon, No. 22, was supplied by the Bristol company, and Snapper Halt was opened between Pilton and Chelfham. In June, a landslide occurred at Dean Steep, between Woody Bay and Lynton, bringing about 50 tons of earth and rock down upon the track. Traffic was disrupted for a day, although the full effect was less serious than it might have been, as the first train had just passed and was trapped on the Lynton side of the blockage. This train was able to keep up a shuttle-service, with others reaching the further side, and passengers had only to walk over the *débris* from one to the other.

In spite of Sir George Newnes's announcement at the opening ceremony, residents of Lynton and Lynmouth petitioned the company in 1901 to extend the line to a more convenient terminus at Lynton, but apart from a vague suggestion by the company about a new approach road, nothing was ever done about this. Because of the high price demanded by the Lynton Water Company, the supply at Lynton was provided from Dean. It was soon found, however, that this was not reliable in dry weather. On the occasions when the supply failed completely a large tank of water was brought to Lynton in an open wagon, and to conserve this meagre supply for essential purposes, even the station lavatories were closed!

Complaints and expressions of alarm were received about the rolling of the carriages, but were met by the explanation that this was due to the transverse springing and, to quote the timetable, 'not the slightest apprehension of danger need be felt'.[3] The rolling stock was, in fact, maintained in excellent condition and well cleaned, to be in keeping with the smartly-dressed staff. The stationmasters and guards were resplendent in frock coats, well covered with gold braid, lettering and buttons, and wore peaked pillbox-type hats. The porters and signalmen wore waistcoats, typical of railway staff at that time. So keen were the management on presenting a clean, tidy undertaking that platelayers were not allowed on the platform at Lynton, but had to slink by on the track.

In 1901 the name of Wooda Bay was changed to Woody Bay. In 1902 two platform wagons, Nos. 20 and 21, were added to the stock, followed by a compo brake, No. 17, next year.

During 1903 an easement was granted to the Ilfracombe Urban District Council to lay water mains under the line near Blackmoor station, where the siding in front of the stables was laid in to cope with the unloading of pipe sections. About this time the company was occupied trying to introduce a £15,000 mortgage, and in 1905 the LSWR took up £20,000 in $4\frac{1}{2}$ per cent debentures, and increased their rebate to the L & BR from 5 per cent to 10 per cent.

In April 1903, Sir George Newnes tried to solve the problem of the unpopularity of the Blackmoor change for horse-coach passengers from Ilfracombe, by operating a motor coach service between Ilfracombe and Blackmoor station. The two motor coaches were open Milnes-Daimler 16 h.p. vehicles, with no windscreens, seating about 20 people in five ascending tiers, like theatre seats. Passengers in the back rows had to climb a six-rung ladder to reach their seats, and there were no doors!

But the experiment was short-lived. To quote a local newspaper: 'One of these cars was travelling at a little over 8 m.p.h. on a bye-road when the police interfered, a prosecution was instituted and a heavy fine inflicted. Sir George Newnes has now decided to stop running the cars over this route.' Sir George referred somewhat bitterly to this setback in a subsequent speech:

> An attempt was made during last year to establish motor car communication between Ilfracombe and Blackmoor Gate in order to develop the Ilfracombe and Lynton traffic. The expense was not undertaken by the railway company but by private enterprise which, of course, the company encouraged. The magistrates, however, in their desire to prevent as far as possible a development of their district, took such steps as to prevent this motor car traffic from being run, and the cars were accordingly sold to the GWR who, it is to be hoped, would find the authorities more reasonable in the districts where they were to be used.

These coaches were used by the GWR to found its Road Transport Department on 3 August 1903 on a service between Helston and the Lizard. Although the GWR is usually given credit for pioneering the use of motor feeder services, the distinction should rightly go to the humble little Lynton & Barnstaple, in co-operation with which Sir George operated his vehicles.

During 1907 a halt was opened at Caffyns to serve the nearby golf course, *Lyn*'s boiler was condemned, and a replacement built by Avonside Works with several modifications. Two years later an

OPENING AND INDEPENDENT DAYS 1898—1923

eight-ton covered brake van, No. 23, was constructed at Pilton yard; about the same time, the other two eight-ton brake vans were modified and the open verandahs were enclosed.

During the years before the First World War, Pilton yard workshops converted all passenger rolling stock from oil-lighting to acetylene, as described in Chapter 8.

Traffic did not develop to the extent which the promoters had optimistically assumed. Much of that from Ilfracombe continued to run direct to Lynton by road, and the Minehead coach services still prospered. In addition, many tourists landed from excursion steamers. But at any rate the railway increased the number of day trippers brought in to Lynton from Barnstaple. Nevertheless, the company still faced complaints about the infrequent trains, though it could only be fairly expected to cater for well-patronised services. For most trains during the year, two coaches were sufficient, and these were augmented on Fridays for people travelling in to Barnstaple market day, to such an extent that the evening down train often ran to six coaches, and was double-headed as far as Bratton Fleming or Blackmoor, where most of the market traffic originated. Here the pilot engine and two or three coaches were detached and returned light to Pilton yard. Naturally, most trains were heavier during the summer season. For one week each September, when the Barnstaple fair was held, trains sometimes ran to the maximum permitted load of nine coaches with two engines. For the winter auction sales of livestock at Woody Bay and Blackmoor Gate about twice a month, special up trains were run, leaving Woody Bay at 3 p.m. or Blackmoor at 3.20 p.m.

In March 1910 the first fatal accident occurred, when Mr W. J. Hart, a platelayer, was killed opening the crossing gates at Braunton Road. The only other fatal accident occurred three years later, on 26 March 1913. Four men had been travelling on a four-ton open wagon, No. 10, which was loaded with ballast, from Bratton Fleming to Chelfham. The wagon gathered speed, the brakes failed to hold it, and on reaching the sharp reverse curves below Chumhill, it left the rails and plunged down a steep bank, killing two of the men. However, the company's accident record was otherwise excellent, and no passenger was ever injured during its existence.

Sir George Newnes died at his home in Lynton on 9 June 1910 and was succeeded as chairman by Sir Thomas Hewitt, K.C.

During 1913, the company added another eight-ton open bogie wagon, No. 24, the last vehicle built while the line was independent. This was also the first year when the company paid a dividend—

½ per cent—which they were able to maintain until 1921.

Just before the war there was a request for an extension to the canopy at Lynton station, and Jones Brothers were asked to make an inexpensive proposition, as funds were low. However, they seem to have been too low even for this, for nothing was done until the Southern made their alterations to the station buildings in the 1920s.

1914—1923

Throughout the First World War the company operated a restricted service. Traffic in pitprops increased to such an extent during this period that the company asked the Festiniog Railway for the loan of flat wagons, but the Welsh company could not help. The passenger traffic fell off, but a basic service of three trains a day in winter and six in summer appears to have been maintained, and it has been recorded that in 1917 there was need for double heading on some market-day trains and during the height of the summer. A few employees joined the Forces, but most of them were considered essential to the line, and after the Kitchener Appeal were issued with badges, showing that they were essential workers.

Sir Thomas Hewitt resigned as chairman in 1919, and was succeeded by Col E. B. Jeune, but the brief period of prosperity was drawing to a close. Competition from motor transport was increasing, and operating costs rising. In 1922 the traffic receipts were £14,511 and the working expenses £14,948. During 1922, negotiations were started for the line to be taken over by the LSWR. At this stage the capital stood at £84,976, with £42,200 loans and debentures. By an agreement of 23 June 1922, the LSWR purchased the line for £39,267, made up of £31,061 for the railway, £7,307 for locomotives and rolling stock, and £899 for the buildings, paying £20,000 in cash and cancelling their first debenture of £20,000. It was then possible to pay off £70 per £100 on first debentures, £65 per £100 on second debentures and 12s per £10 to shareholders. The Southern Railway Act 1923 gave the powers for the acquisition, and the final agreement was reached in March 1923, the Lynton & Barnstaple Railway ceasing to exist independently on 1 July 1923.

CHAPTER 4

Southern Days 1923-1935

NEW OWNERSHIP

Under the Railway Act of 1921 the LSWR passed into the control of the Southern Railway from 1 January 1923. The Railway Act did not apply to jointly-owned lines, or narrow-gauge railways, and each of the Big Four companies proceeded to take special powers to absorb such lines. The draft plan for absorbing the Lynton & Barnstaple Railway had been reached with the LSWR in June 1922, and this was ratified under the Southern Railway Act in March 1923, when the last board meeting of the independent company was held.

Sir Frank Newnes presided and referred to the death of Sir Thomas Hewitt earlier in the year. This final meeting was also attended by Sir Edward Mountain, Mr C. E. Roberts Chanter and Mr C. E. Drewett, and Sir Frank paid tribute to the 22 years' service given by Mr Drewett as general manager. Mr Drewett retired with the take-over, but continued to live in Barnstaple. It is curious to recall that this man, who had given such service to the company, started his L & BR career on six months' trial, with leave of absence from his previous employers, the LSWR.

Signs of change of ownership soon became evident. The Southern Railway decided that money had to be spent on the line if it were to have a chance of survival. First attention was given to the arrears of maintenance which lack of money had forced upon the old company. Fresh sleepers were laid throughout, closer together than the old ones, and the former rail spikes were replaced by bolts and clips, with bedplates between the rail and the sleepers. As an experiment, concrete sleepers were used, but were found to be less resilient than wooden ones, accentuating the noisy running which is characteristic of narrow-gauge operation. The experiment was not extended, but some concrete sleepers remained in use at stations and on straight lengths of track near Blackmoor Gate.

As far as is known, no new rails were laid, but one length of track adjacent to Pilton Wharf at Barnstaple was relaid with standard chaired track, as was the track over the large inspection pit at Pilton yard. Several curves, particularly near Barbrook, were re-aligned, the entire line re-ballasted, and the fencing repaired, a number of concrete posts being cast in Bratton Fleming station yard. Some of the old wooden signal-posts were replaced by new ones of LSWR lattice-type pattern, or SR standard type made from rails. South Western pattern signal arms also replaced the Midland type used by the old company. (Eventually there was one upper quadrant signal on the line, to the up home at Woody Bay.)

The rolling stock had been kept in good condition, and although it was all renumbered into the Southern system, repainting was slow. Some of the goods vehicles were painted with SR initials, but retained their L & BR numbers for a time.

The station buildings at Lynton were enlarged, and altered internally, part of the stationmaster's accommodation being absorbed into the station offices, and a new bungalow home built on the bank opposite the station. At about the same time a canteen was built for the staff, alongside the engine-shed at Pilton yard, and Parracombe Halt received a new waiting shelter.

The Southern turned its attention to the rolling stock, and in 1925 added a further Manning Wardle locomotive, which was delivered in Southern colours and bore the name *Lew*. Some of the first-class compartments were converted to thirds. As their turn came, the other locomotives and rolling stock were overhauled and repainted at Pilton yard, the boilers of the Manning Wardles being sent to Eastleigh for major repair, this being about the only work which could not be done in the Pilton shops. As there was a spare boiler for these engines, it was a relatively easy matter to use this as a replacement and then to send the displaced one to Eastleigh for overhaul, after which this would become the spare. Late in 1928 *Lyn* (which had no spare boiler) was shipped to Eastleigh for a major overhaul, and returned to Barnstaple in January 1929.

While being overhauled, many of the third-class compartments had thin upholstered cushions fitted to the original wooden seats. In 1926 the Southern Railway bought two cranes from Messrs George Cohen & Co. The following year a match truck was built at Lancing, and this and one crane were kept at Pilton yard to deal with breakdowns. The other crane stood on its own track alongside the shed road at Lynton, where it was used for yard work. One of these cranes was to achieve notoriety in 1936, a year after the line closed, when it collided with the footbridge at Braunton Road Crossing. During 1927 four eight-ton open bogie wagons and four

BARNSTAPLE TOWN
(11) *From the Transhipment siding, 1898*
(12) *Awaiting the connection*
(13) *'Exe' waiting to shunt*

OUTSIDE BARNSTAPLE
(14) *View looking towards exchange sidings*
(15) *The Transhipment siding—'Lyn' returning from Eastleigh, 1929*

PILTON YARD

(16) *'Lyn' on the carriage shed road, c. 1906*
(17) *Trains prepared for the opening on 11 May 1898*

PILTON—CHELFHAM
(18) *A general view of Pilton in Southern days*
(19) *Derailment near Snapper, c. 1922*

eight-ton bogie covered vans were built for the line by J. & F. Howard of Bedford.

Other improvements followed. The timetable was augmented and restored to something like its pre-war standard. Summer Sunday working was resumed, with excursion trains run to connect with standard-gauge trains from Ilfracombe, Torrington, Plymouth, Yeovil, and other places. On one summer Sunday during the middle 1920s, four engines and every one of the 17 coaches were pressed into service. Nor was publicity overlooked entirely by the parent company. Several references appeared in Southern Railway publications and advertisements, and in one book entitled *Devon and Cornish Days*, a colourful journalistic account of a journey over the line was included. It can be appreciated that this particular guide book was not written by a railwayman when one reads 'the bumptious little engine gives vent to a falsetto shriek of pride on approaching and leaving stations'.

THE BEGINNING OF THE END

But despite all the Southern's efforts, by 1931 the writing was on the wall; times of some of the Southern National bus services were included in the Railway timetable. During the following year economies in operation resulted in the removal of the passing loop at Bratton Fleming and of one of the sidings in the yard there. One of the sidings at Blackmoor Gate had been similarly removed in 1930. This necessitated several adjustments in the timetables, and attempts were made to speed up the service. To encourage local winter patronage the locomotives and six of the coaches were fitted with steam heating in 1933, replacing the old metal footwarmers.

In spite of all these efforts, the line continued to lose ground. In 1925, the company issued 72,000 tickets; in 1934 the figure had fallen to 32,000. The working loss in 1927 was £5,900 and thereafter never fell below £5,000. After the 1927 loss, Mr E. Cox, traffic manager of the Southern, and several other officials visited the district to make a special attempt to stimulate more traffic. But there was little hope against increasing road competition. The improvement of the Barnstaple to Lynton road, including a new length avoiding two steep hills at Parracombe, further reduced the line's competitiveness. Few local people used the line.

All the criticisms voiced when the line was opened now carried much more weight, but the physical limitations made improvements impossible. The lack of convenient connections at Barnstaple with the GWR caused more people to use the bus from Minehead to Lynton. Not surprisingly, Ilfracombe excursionists went direct by motor coach to Lynton rather than change trains. The railway remained a favourite with holidaymakers, even motorists taking occasional trips on it. Six or more coaches were still provided during the height of the season, but this was all too short and did not provide enough fat for the lean winter months.

The Southern continued to operate a full service until 1934, when it started to move some of the older employees elsewhere on the system. In 1935 it was faced with permanent way renewals which would have cost £2,000 a year for six years. It was then decided to close the line at the end of the summer season.

FIRST NEWS OF THE CLOSURE

The official announcement shocked the whole of North Devon, and particularly Lynton, where the decision was made known in answer to a request for a halt at Barbrook, about a mile out of the terminus. Suddenly, everyone loved the railway. Lynton Urban District Council, alarmed lest the closure should harm the fortunes of the twin towns, protested vigorously. It complained that journey time was too long; that departure times from Lynton were inconvenient (9.25 a.m. was too early and 12.42 p.m. too late for day trippers); that the 12.42 p.m. meant lunching early or going without, whereas the 2 p.m. bus offered a more convenient connection with the London train; reference was also made to the poor connection with the GWR at Barnstaple, in particular with the afternoon train from the Midlands which, by reaching Barnstaple just after the last train for Lynton had left, forced passengers to travel *via* Minehead. The desirability of a station bus at Lynton was mentioned, but one practically-minded councillor remarked that in the absence of passengers, this need was not apparent. Despite other complaints about slow goods deliveries, the Council felt that the line was indispensable, and convened a meeting of local interests to discuss the situation.

Accordingly, a conference was called for 11 April at the Castle, Barnstaple. It was attended by representatives of Barnstaple Town Council, Lynton Urban Council, Lynton Advertising Association, Barnstaple and District Chamber of Commerce, and the parish councils of High Bray, Swimbridge and Brendon. After thorough discussion and consideration of the introduction of a diesel locomotive to reduce operating costs, or, since the track was due for renewal, the replacement by standard gauge to eliminate the time and cost of transhipment, the meeting considered suggestions for achieving economy of operation.

It was agreed to ask Sir Basil Peto, the local M.P., who had already expressed his willingness to help, to join a delegation to meet the Southern. But the delegates from Lynton had already struck a damning blow at their own cause, for they had all travelled to the Barnstaple conference by car! It is not surprising, therefore, that the request for a meeting was not very enthusiastically received by Sir Herbert Walker, the Southern's general manager, who 'felt that no useful purpose would be served by the deputation travelling to London, as the Company's decision had been arrived at only after very careful consideration of all the factors'. He excused himself from the proposed meeting, pleading a prior engagement. However, the deputation was duly met by the traffic manager, Mr E. S. Cox, who listened attentively to their suggestions, but could not be moved from the decision.

Up to this time, the local opinion had been that the company was not serious in its intention, and one councillor had even suggested that the announcement of closure had merely been a scare to get more people to use the railway. Now, however, there was no doubt that the Southern meant to close the line.

Ironically, in the spring of 1935, *Exe* emerged from the Pilton shops after a general overhaul and repaint, and the summer train services were speeded up, the practice of collecting tickets at Woody Bay, which often took five minutes, being discontinued. During the holiday season, almost record loads were carried, particularly in August Bank Holiday week, when one train of nine coaches took over 400 passengers into Lynton.

As the day for closure drew nearer, the Lynton line became a talking-point throughout North Devon; there were wild speculations that some local interest or eccentric millionaire might yet take over the railway. At the eleventh hour, a new surge of hope ran through the district when on 26 September the clerk to the Lynton Council announced that he had received an anonymous telephone call suggesting that under the 1895 Act the company was obliged to maintain and operate the line in perpetuity, as there were two mandatory clauses, the first relating to Woody Bay station which 'the Company shall construct and forever efficiently maintain' and the other that the line 'shall be constructed and maintained as a two foot gauge line'. It is not clear, however, to what extent the Southern Railway Act of 1923 superseded this.

The clerk was authorised to obtain counsel's opinion, the outcome of which was a suggested course of action, which, if the Council was unsuccessful, would cost not more than £500. At a specially called meeting, the ratepayers of Lynton and Lynmouth were asked to authorise the council to risk this sum, but a mandate was refused by a narrow majority. In any case, the council was now faced with a *fait accompli*, for by this time the last train had already run.

Bridge 39 devoid of track

CHAPTER 5

Closing, Sale and After

THE LAST TRAIN FROM LYNTON

The morning of Sunday 29 September 1935 was fair, and four locomotives and all passenger rolling stock were prepared for this, the last day of operation. The last train was a connection for a half-day excursion from Ilfracombe and Torrington, scheduled to leave Barnstaple Town at 11.50 a.m. About 300 people presented themselves, and nine coaches, behind *Yeo*, with *Lew* as pilot, proved sufficient. The journey out to Lynton was not a particularly fast one, 4m. 28s. being spent at Chelfham for water, and 4m. 37s. at Parracombe for the same purpose. Stops of 2m. 19s. at Bratton Fleming, 4m. 32s. at Blackmoor, and 1m. 32s. at Woody Bay were also recorded. A minute and a second just short of Lynton, to allow *Lew* to be detached and run into the bay road, gave a total journey time of 94m. 29s., of which 76m. were running-time.

The return journey was scheduled to leave Lynton at 7.55 p.m., arriving at Barnstaple Town 9.22 p.m. The train was joined by the chairman and several members of the Lynton Council, about 30 residents, and the town band. The last train pulled out of Lynton to the strains of 'Auld Lang Syne', cheering from the crowds, whistling from the engines and explosions from detonators placed on the track. The Lynton party left the train at Blackmoor, where the station was crowded to capacity and the train stopped for 8 minutes. Finally, after a 3-minute stop at Bratton Fleming the train reached Barnstaple Town 15 minutes late at 9.37 p.m., having taken 98m. 58s., of which 83 minutes were running-time. About a thousand people had gathered in the rain at North Walk to pay their last respects, and after more flashlight photographs, it was with a measure of relief that the crews were able to take their train back to Pilton yard, as stocks of coal and water were running low. On the following morning, the final act was performed when the stationmaster placed a wreath sent by a Woody Bay resident, and inscribed 'In loving memory', on the stop-block at Barnstaple Town.

THE SALE

Once the last train had run, the Southern Railway lost no time in sorting out what was going to be of use elsewhere on their system, and what could be sold. Some machines from the workshop found a use at Eastleigh, and were moved there *via* the transfer siding. All rolling stock was marshalled into Pilton yard, and photographs show that even the running roads were used. The company undertook to remove the track between Lynton and milepost 15½ themselves before the sale, and the demolition train behind *Yeo* completed this task on 8 November, when it left 15½ milepost at 12.2 p.m., and with a stop at Parracombe for water and at various points to pick up guard rails, arrived at Pilton at 1.34 p.m. By this time all the equipment had acquired lot numbers.

The sale was held in the carriage shed on Wednesday 13 November 1935. The large crowd present included sentimental souvenir hunters as well as those with commercial motives. Before bidding began, it was announced that the nameplates of the locomotives were being preserved. Some were subsequently kept by the Southern at Eastleigh, some at York Railway Museum. The remaining set passed into the hands of Mr W. E. Heywood of Weston-super-Mare, who has now given them to the Railway Board's Historical Records.

The first four lots comprised track from 15½mp. to 11½mp., 11½mp. to 7½mp., 7½mp. to 3mp., and 3mp. to Barnstaple Town. Bidding rose to 2s a yard, when they were withdrawn for subsequent sale privately. Lot 6 was *Lew*, the newest and reputedly the best of the locomotives, which fetched £52. Lots 7 and 8 were *Yeo* and *Taw*, which each fetched £50, but Lot 9, *Exe*, which was fitted with a steel firebox (unlike her sisters and the spare boiler, which had copper fireboxes), only fetched £34. Lot 10 was the spare boiler, which realised £20. Lots 11 and 12 were spares for the Manning Wardle engines, and Lot 13, which was *Lyn* with her spares, went down for £50. With the exception of *Lew* all the locomotives were sold to Messrs John Cashmore Ltd., steel and scrap metal merchants. Lots 14 to 30 were the seventeen coaches, which realised from £10 to £13 10s. There then followed the goods rolling stock in Lots 31 to 62. Prices ranged from £6 10s to £9 10s for bogie goods wagons and vans, while the four-wheel open trucks fetched £3 15s each. Lots 63 and 64 comprised various carriage and wagon spares, and enthusiasts paid 7s 6d for a first-class carriage mat. Lots 65, 66 and 67 consisted of the two portable cranes, which fetched £30 and

£29, and the jib truck, which fetched £6 10s.

The remaining lots—over 130 of them—consisted of such varied articles as tanks, handcranes, jib-cranes, signal cabins, lamp-posts, signal rods, a five-ton weighbridge (which realised £29), lathes, benches and other workshop equipment. The turntable, together with a signal, went to the Romney, Hythe & Dymchurch Railway. Certain lots were sold subject to their being removed by fixed dates. Bridges and bridge materials, rails over the two level crossings and the level crossing gates were excluded from the sale.

Demolition began soon after the sale. *Yeo, Exe, Taw* and *Lyn* were soon reduced to four piles of scrap at Pilton yard, although the wooden cab of *Lyn*, being useless to a scrap merchant, was sold to one of the drivers for use as a garden shed. The wooden bodies of the carriages and wagons were stripped off and burned, only the metal underframes and running gear remaining intact.

The track was removed by Mr S. Castle, of Plymouth, who used *Lew* with a train of a bogie van and three wagons. Two of these wagons were coal wagons and were used for carrying sleepers, the third, a platform wagon, carried rails. Starting where the Southern had left off, at milepost 15½, he lifted and transferred it to the main line at the transfer siding, where the narrow-gauge track was slewed and raised to make the operation easier.

Demolition proceeded rather more slowly than laid down in the sale conditions, but the track was removed as far as the down end of Pilton yard by the summer of 1936. Towards the end of September *Lew* was loaded on to a standard-gauge wagon at the transfer siding and taken away for overhaul, before taking a new lease of life on a coffee plantation in Brazil, where she is believed to have given good service until recent years. A few weeks later most of the steel underframes were taken away to accompany her on her transatlantic journey. Only four 4-wheeled open wagons remained, on which the last materials were wheeled round to the transfer siding. The rails between Pilton yard and Barnstaple Town survived until the summer of 1937, when they too were lifted and the four wagons disappeared.

The signal cabin at Barnstaple Town, which had been in use until *Lew* departed, was demolished in 1938, but station buildings elsewhere were left derelict, later to be sold by private treaty. Bratton Fleming fetched £100, Blackmoor £700, Woody Bay £425, and Lynton £475. From time to time road improvements have removed some of the features of the line, notably the bridge carrying the main road over the line between Snapper and Chelfham, and a similar main road bridge near Woody Bay, where part of the deep cutting was also filled in. Later the main road bridges at Blackmoor Gate and Dean Steep vanished for similar reasons, together with a length of cutting and earthworks at the latter point. Altogether, the Devon County Council took over responsibility for the maintenance of 12 road bridges.

TODAY

So to today. The Lynton line platform at Barnstaple Town station is unaltered, as is the transfer dock, although with this station earmarked for closure, it may not be there much longer. The spur of the main-line transfer siding is now a catch-point trap. The curve round to the wharf can still be seen and forms part of a car park. A youth movement hut sits roughly where the track passed the wharf, and the level crossing gates beyond are still in position. The offices at Pilton yard house a woollen goods and fellmonger's business; the old canteen is now a salt store. A builder's merchant occupies the loco, carriage and goods sheds, which are intact, but only the foundations of the signal box remain.

Further down the line at Snapper, the remains of coach 6991 can be seen, but 6993, which was a little farther along and was used as a hen house, has been dismantled and moved to the Festiniog Railway. After it had been stripped down at Boston Lodge Works, near Portmadoc, the chassis was pushed and rolled gently out of the shop without effort, a great testimony to the maintenance it received in early days. The coach has been completely rebuilt to conform to the Festiniog loading gauge and after 25 years is now running again, as a buffet car.

Chelfham viaduct is still intact and, minus its parapet walls, stands gaunt above the countryside. Lancey Brook viaduct did its last service as a practice target for Territorials, who blew it up, and the horseshoe curve at the head of the valley near Westlandpound has disappeared beneath the waters of a reservoir. At Blackmoor, the station buildings have been turned into a café by the nearby hotel, and the stables have been converted into cottages. The station buildings at Chelfham, Bratton Fleming and Woody Bay are used as private houses, and part of Parracombe embankment was washed away at the time of the Lynmouth disaster a few years ago. And so to Lynton, where Station House is still so called, while the goods shed has been turned into a pair of cottages. Next to the original stationmaster's house on the bank opposite the platforms another house has appeared. The engine shed has gone to make way for a new house, and the foundations of the groundframe mark a flower-bed. Nearby, a buzzing sound comes from the coaling stage, which now houses three beehives.

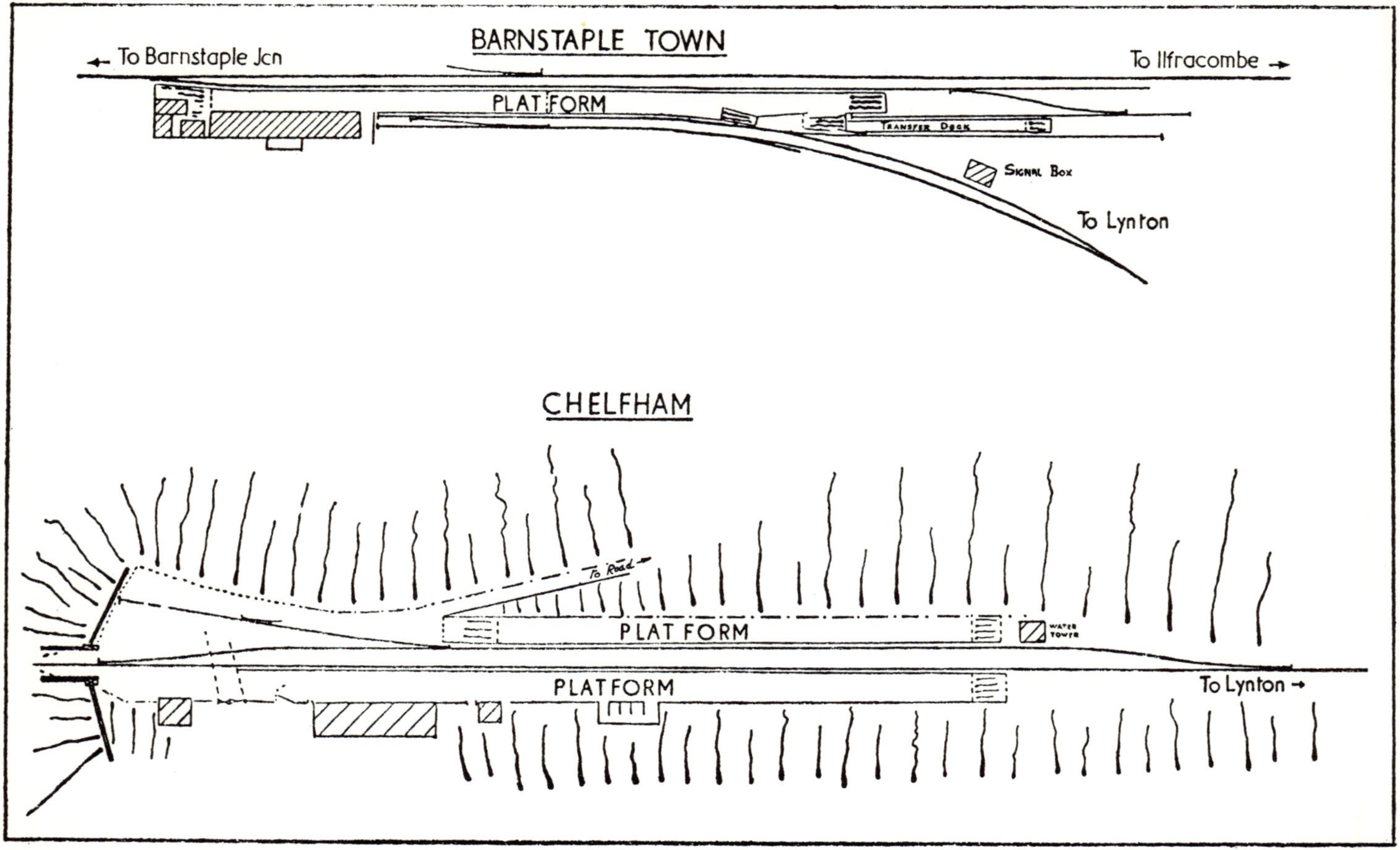
BARNSTAPLE TOWN
← To Barnstaple Jcn
To Ilfracombe →
PLAT FORM
TRANSFER DOCK
SIGNAL BOX
To Lynton
CHELFHAM
To Road →
PLAT FORM
WATER TOWER
PLATFORM
To Lynton →

Layout of Barnstaple and Chelfham

CHAPTER 6

The Route

BARNSTAPLE TO SNAPPER HALT

Most travellers began their acquaintance with the Lynton & Barnstaple at Barnstaple Town. The LSWR Ilfracombe line, sandwiched between the town and the river Taw, was single at this point and one platform was sufficient for both railways. The narrow gauge trains were accommodated in a bay on the north side, having 326 ft of platform face. The run-round loop was extended beyond the release crossover, and the 'dead-end' thus formed was often used to store a spare carriage which might be added to down trains. There was space for an arrival platform, but this was never built.

At the down end of the platform, the goods transhipment siding branched from the platform road and ran alongside a loading stage parallel with a complementary standard-gauge siding, and part of this platform was used, latterly at any rate, as a coal stage for the Lynton locomotives. At the same end of the passenger platform a water column was provided. Points and signals, the latter comprising the down starter and the up home, were operated from a ground frame in the glazed and weatherboarded signal cabin between the running line and the siding.

As the running line left the platform it curved very sharply to the right, bringing it alongside the tree-fringed bank of the Yeo, on whose opposite bank there was usually some shipping activity at Rolle Quay. The bustling energy displayed on leaving the station diminished as the train ground round the long curve, and since the usual humorous idiosyncrasies were attributed to the railway by the locals, the uninitiated passenger might be forgiven for thinking that the engine was already 'going off the boil'; in fact, it was being eased for the beginning of an eight m.p.h. speed restriction indicated by a board on the right of the line. This, and a double-arm signal, marked the approach to Braunton Road level crossing, which was gated, and provided with a footbridge for pedestrians.

Just beyond was the two-lever frame controlling the facing points

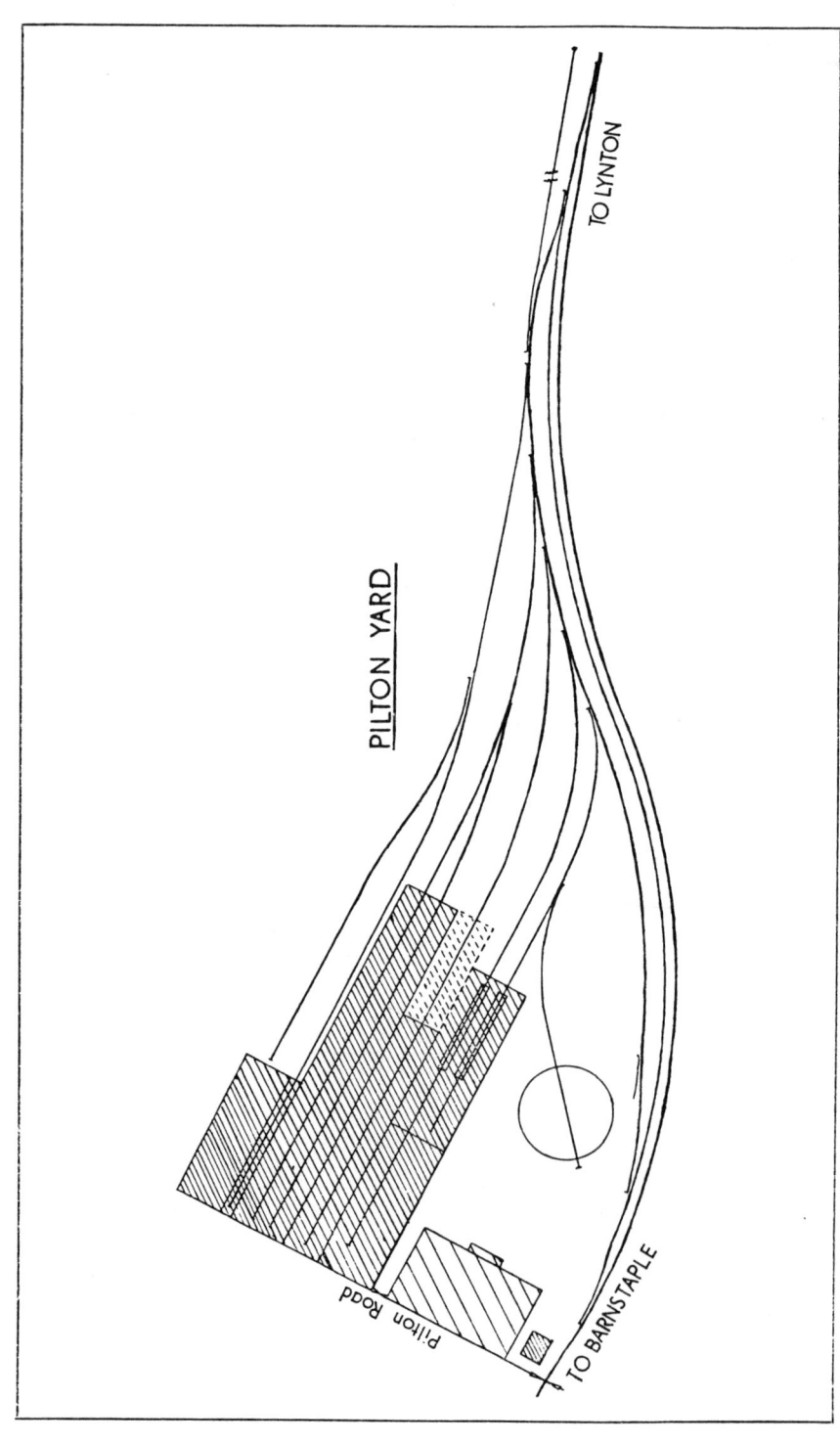

of the Quay siding on the left. Here the railway turned sharply away from the river and soon crossed Pilton Road, similarly equipped to the crossing at Braunton Road, and entered Pilton yard. The gates at both crossings were hand-operated, being locked by levers in Pilton Bridge signal cabin and protected by the same double-arm signal, which was also the Pilton yard down home, and in the up direction by the Pilton up starter. These were operated from Pilton signal box, situated immediately beyond the second level crossing and controlling the entrance to Pilton yard.

This was the main depot of the railway and the operational headquarters of the old company, whose general offices were on the left. The running lines formed a passing loop and traversed a long reverse curve through the yard; running parallel on the left was the yard loop from which branched all the roads serving the various sheds.

The locomotive shed was a corrugated-sheeted structure having two roads, each with an inspection pit between the rails. The right-hand road extended through the shed into the workshop. Outside the shed, this same road was carried over a wide inspection pit on steel joists, heavier section rails being used to span the opening. It is easy to imagine how the more corpulent enginemen must have blessed this amenity. The original flat-bottomed rails were replaced in later years by standard chaired bullhead ones. A further siding branched from the left-hand shed road to serve the coal stage and turntable in front of the offices. The water column stood near the yard loop opposite the coal stage. Between the offices and the running shed was a small yard containing a smithy, sand ovens and a store shed.

Between the locomotive shed and the carriage shed proper, there was a single road shed, originally an open siding, whose innermost depth formed the carriage repair and paint shop, the outer end being used for carriage storage. This shed bore the number '1' on its gable end, together with a warning notice 'shunt with care'. The two-road carriage shed was a substantial stone building of considerable length. Goods were accommodated in two sidings on the right of the carriage shed, the one nearest to it terminating in a small goods shed. The goods yard was fairly spacious and had a weighbridge for road vehicles, and a set of sheer legs with blocks and tackle for handling heavy loads.

A crossover now reconnected the yard loop with the running lines, but the loop extended for some distance to form a useful shunting spur and storage siding. The running lines, too, became single again. The points at this end of the yard were operated from a ground frame controlled by a locking lever in Pilton Bridge signal box. All the siding points on the yard loop were controlled by local weighted hand-levers.

Beyond the yard there were no speed restrictions, and the train passed between the back gardens of houses for a few hundred yards before crossing a mill leat, and in quick succession passed under a minor road, over the leat again and then over the Yeo. It was now under the right-hand slopes of the valley, with the river immediately alongside on the left. Here the passengers in the up trains were treated to an ear-splitting performance upon the engine whistle, warning the gatesmen at the level crossings. The line now crossed the river again but kept to the right of the valley, climbing a short gradient of 1 in 55 which eased after about half-a-mile to 1 in 528. The discerning passenger might catch a distant glimpse of Goodleigh church tower and the main road from Barnstaple descending the hill on the right, before the train rounded a sharp curve and stopped at Snapper Halt which, though at Yeotown, is named after a former inn about a quarter of a mile further along the main road. Passenger accommodation on the right of the line consisted of a ground level platform with a small waiting shelter. A footpath led up to the road.

SNAPPER HALT TO BRATTON FLEMING

Above Snapper the valley narrows considerably, and becomes typical of the district in its winding course and wooded interlocking sides; consequently the railway made several changes in direction between Snapper and the far side of Chelfham. Just north of Snapper it crossed the river again and reached the left side of the valley, the gradient steepening, followed by a further right-hand curve and a short descent at a gentler gradient, crossing the river for the last time on a substantial twin arch stone bridge to regain the right-hand side of the valley, where it was to stay for many miles. Now, passing under a minor road bridge—known as Collar Bridge[4]—the line began to climb the ruling gradient of 1 in 50 which extended with only short variations almost to Blackmoor. Another long right-hand curve brought the railway round a shoulder of the valley and under the main road, the direction meanwhile changing to east.

With road and river now on the left, the line continued to climb through woods, and Chelfham viaduct could be seen through the trees, the eight arches of Marland bricks standing some 70 ft above the valley floor on masonry piers, with a small cluster of cottages at its feet. After about half a mile the line turned north again and emerged from sylvan surroundings to pass Chelfham down home signal and cross the viaduct, whose high parapets, originally topped with iron handrails, denied the passenger all but a distant view up the Stoke Rivers valley on the right and of Youlston Wood on the left, before entering Chelfham station.

Perched upon the hillside at the junction of two valleys and among pleasant wooded surroundings, Chelfham was the most picturesque station on the line. It had a passing loop and a short siding trailing from the down line to intersect the down platform, an arrangement necessitated by the narrow hillside formation. The siding was rarely used, except perhaps for an odd coal wagon. As at all the stations except Barnstaple Town, the platforms were at rail level. The simple buildings were on the up side and comprised a small stone booking office and waiting room, and a wooden shed housing the ground frame. The approach road curved steeply down the hillside to join the Stoke Rivers road under the viaduct, and from the down platform the footpath for Loxhore led through the trees down to the main road. There was a water tank mounted on stanchions, from which engines of down trains could replenish their tanks.

Continuing to climb through the woods for another half-mile or so, the railway now made a further change in course where it left the Yeo and turned north east along the valley of an unnamed tributary, at the same time taking to the open hillside with a brief view up the Yeo valley towards Loxhore. With the riverside meadows and wooded hillsides behind, it now entered a district of hillside farmsteads, a tortuous course taking it past that at Chumhill and over several culverts before reaching Lancey Brook viaduct, 28 ft high, a curving structure of eight steel spans on masonry piers, with timber deck and iron handrails. Another small wood was now passed and, on the right, a small quarry from which ballast was obtained in the early days. This heralded the approach to Bratton Fleming station, where the train passed a water tank on its right before drawing up at the platform. No doubt, because of the labour involved in refilling this tank by hand pump and the delay of several minutes outside the station, drivers usually dispensed with water here. By leaving Chelfham with the tanks full, it was normally possible to reach Blackmoor or Parracombe without replacement.

Bratton Fleming station was simple, like Chelfham, but larger, and like Chelfham it was very pretty, especially when the roses and hydrangeas were in bloom. It was the stationmaster here, Mr Mintern, who in 1899 first won the annual prize of £5 awarded by Sir George Newnes for the station with the best-kept flower beds.

Here also, because it was on a hill, the goods siding intersected the down platform. In the hope of stimulating slate traffic, a second

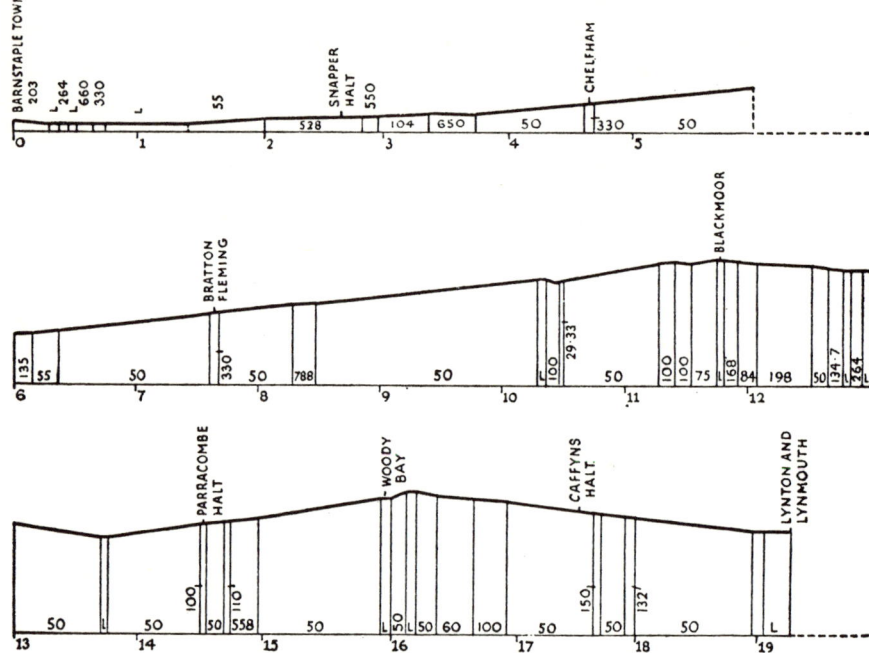

siding was added in the early years of the century, but it was removed in February 1932. All the station buildings were on the up platform, whence a path led to the nearby lane and village.

BRATTON FLEMING TO PARRACOMBE HALT

As the line left Bratton Fleming station, a sharp right-hand curve brought it into a rock cutting and under two minor roads[5] before it entered upon a horseshoe embankment 40 ft high. By means of this it negotiated Bratton Valley, crossing two small streams and the culvert which was built to provide an avenue of escape for the hunted deer. Having travelled in three different directions in about

AROUND CHELFHAM—1
(20) *The Viaduct*
(21) *Winter trains crossing*

AROUND CHELFHAM—2
(22) *'Taw' climbing through the woods*
(23) *Climbing from Chelfham with the last train*

CHELFHAM—BRATTON

(24) *Double-headed train at Chumhill, c. 1922*
(25) & (26) *Autumn and spring in the Bratton Valley*

BRATTON FLEMING

(27) *Looking South, 1898*
(28) *In Edwardian days*
(29) *'Lew' awaiting departure for Barnstaple, c. 1929*

half a mile, it resumed a generally northerly course. For a mile or two after Bratton Fleming, seven hillside farms were passed in fairly quick succession—Beara, Southacott, Knightacott, Narracott, Sprecott, Hunnacott and South Thorne—and the network of narrow lanes which linked them crossed either above or below the railway, which was carried successively on embankments or in cuttings. In two of the latter, streams were carried over the line by means of aqueducts. The difficulties encountered in laying out the line could be easily appreciated from the abundance of curves and earthworks, and near milepost $10\frac{1}{4}$ the gradient suddenly changed to a short descent at 1 in 100 followed by an equally short climb at 1 in 29.33 before the ruling gradient was resumed near milepost $10\frac{1}{2}$.

The head of the valley was now reached, and was traversed by another horseshoe curve leading to Westlandpound—the halfway house of the old Barnstaple to Lynton pack-horse road. A cutting through the ridge brought the railway on a falling gradient to another hillside location high above the headwaters of a further tributary of the Yeo, and climbing was resumed (at 1 in 75) on approaching Blackmoor station. Bracken and furze now showed travellers how near to the moorland they were. The line had now reached a high elevation and was exposed to gales which once derailed some carriages in Westlandpound cutting.

Half a mile later the train came into the large and important Blackmoor station. On the up platform were the chalet-type station buildings, and on the same side of the line the goods yard with its two sidings and stores. Here also were the stables for the horses which brought the coaches from Ilfracombe. A further siding on the down side was probably intended either for the storage of a spare passenger carriage, for the Ilfracombe traffic to Lynton, or to lighten any down train from which sufficient passengers had alighted by the time Blackmoor was reached. It does not appear to have been used much and was removed in 1930. On the down platform was a large tank[6] from which water was piped to a water column on the up platform.

Passing under the main road at Rowley Cross, at the watershed between Kentisbury Down on the west and Rowley Down on the east, the line now began to descend towards the Heddon Valley, skirting the north-west slopes of Rowley Down. After a mile or so the road to Parracombe was carried over the line, while the newer by-pass continued alongside, and yet another horseshoe curve over Parracombe embankment marked the resumption of the ascending 1 in 50 gradient. From the left-hand windows, passengers could see

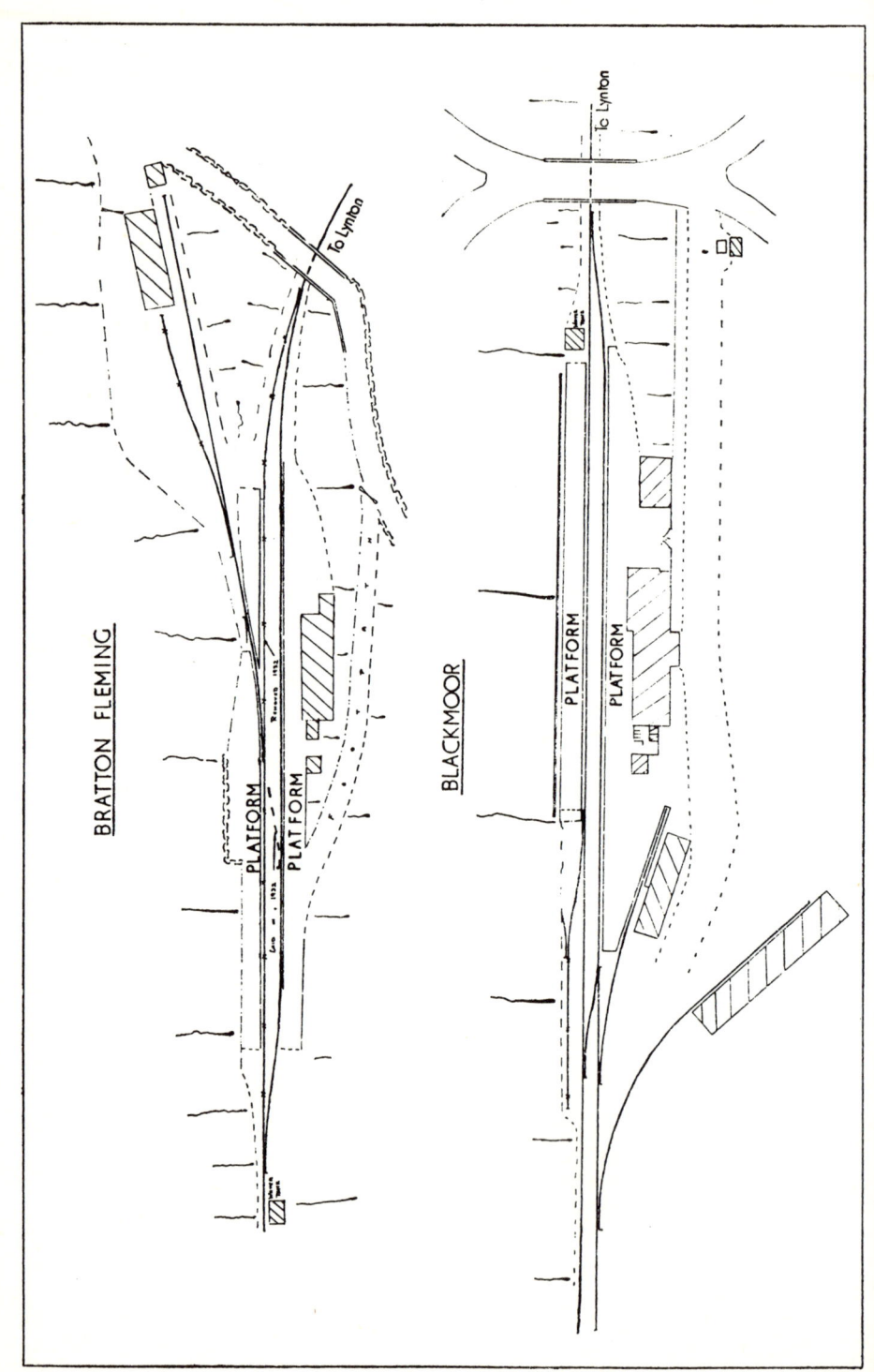

the village of Parracombe from three points of the compass, and more distantly the twin summits of the Great and Little Hangman Hills overlooking the sea at Combe Martin, while less than two miles behind were the central highlands of Exmoor, known as The Chains. At Parracombe Halt, the train drew up alongside a water tank near the Saxon church of St Petrock. In the early days, the rector, the Rev J. F. Chanter, helped to produce a flash of colour along the lineside by scattering flower seeds from the carriage window.

This fair-sized village, served more closely by the railway than any other intermediate community, was provided with less station facilities. This emphasised the lack of local need for a railway, and passengers were so few that the station duties were discharged by the guard long before the locomotive had replenished its tanks.

PARRACOMBE TO LYNTON

Passing under the church lane, the line continued to climb round the shoulder of Parracombe Common, with the main road higher up on the right. The road from the village to Lynton, climbing steeply, passed overhead, as did the road to Hunters Inn and Heddons Mouth further on. On the left there was a fine view into the wooded depths of the Heddon Valley and across to Martinhoe Common, a truly moorland scene, abounding in rabbits and at its best when the heather was in bloom. Woody Bay station layout was similar to that at Blackmoor, though there was only one goods siding, and the chalet-type buildings were smaller. Like so many other factors in this railway, Woody Bay (known before 1901 as 'Wooda Bay') failed, alas, to justify the optimism of the promoters, and the station became little more than a convenient point for the collection of tickets on the down trains.

The summit of the railway, 980 ft above sea level, was reached in a deep cutting just after Woody Bay station, where the main road again crossed the line, and a few yards further on, the lane to Woolhanger also bridged the cutting, whose rock walls may inspire a thought for the unfortunate Mr Nuttall. The line was now back on the hillside. On the left hand were slopes, with a tributary of the West Lyn river on the right and, beyond it, magnificent views over West Ilkerton Common to the heights of Exmoor. After descending a gradient of 1 in 50, the train paused briefly at Caffyns Halt, where the platform and shelter were on the right. Passing first under a lane leading to West Ilkerton, then under the main road, which fell

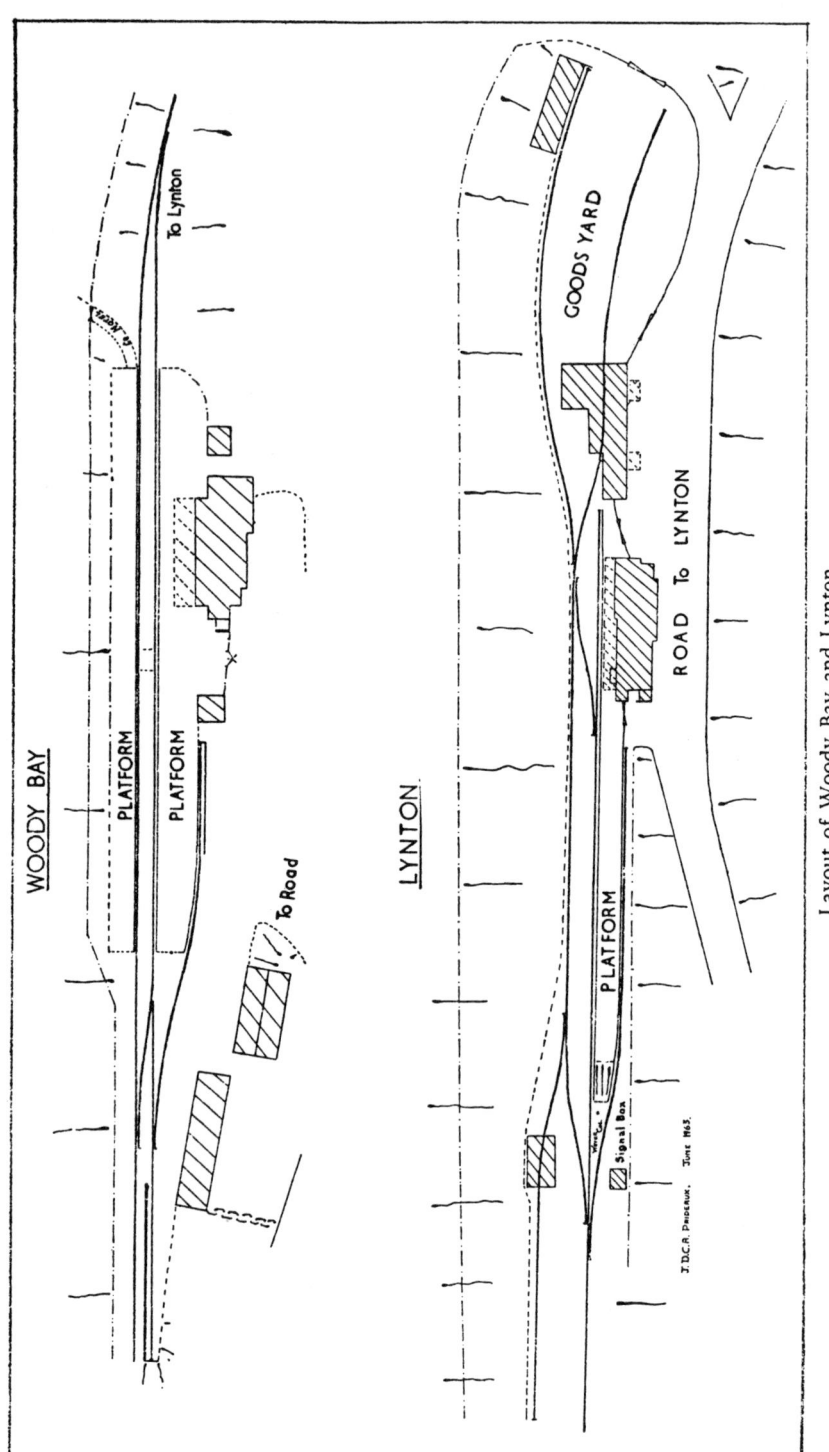

Layout of Woody Bay and Lynton

THE ROUTE 61

steeply to the valley floor, the line curved sharply east at Dean Steep and held this course for a further half-mile to Barbrook, where it again turned north, being about 150 ft up the slope. From here the passenger could see the Bristol Channel, and if discerning enough might spot Lynton station before the curving hillside hid both scenes. The train was now passing through a hillside wood, the first since Bratton Fleming, and while still admiring the wooded depths of the valley, the passenger suddenly found that he had arrived at Lynton station, 19¼ miles from Barnstaple and 700 ft above sea level.

This station was laid out in keeping with its importance as a terminus, even down to a bookstall, and was completed just before the line was opened. There was a large goods shed and goods office, and a running shed for one locomotive. At first, Lynton had a double slip point between the two platform roads, the main line and the shed spur. Shortly after the line opened, this point was replaced by simple points, a fresh access to the locomotive shed being provided by the runround loop, through the other end of the shed. The original spur beyond the shed was left in position, and contained an inspection pit and coaling stage. Ashes were often cleared on to this line. About the same time, the crossover at the other end of the station was reversed to simplify shunting (see chapter 9), and an extra siding was laid behind the goods shed. The buildings were enlarged and altered internally by the Southern during the late 'twenties, and the new bungalow for the stationmaster was built on the bank outside.

Such was Lynton's 'invisible terminus'. No one who has toiled up the long hill from the town in pouring rain or under the midsummer sun will deny the justification of the residents' complaints against the 'carefully selected site'.

Note: The layout plans reproduced in this chapter are based on an LSWR official survey of 1922. They are *not* to scale and the authors recommend that they should only be used for accurate work in conjunction with photographs and the dimensions given in Appendix 3. In particular the alignment of Lynton goods shed road is incorrectly shown on the diagram.

CHAPTER 7

Locomotives

LOCOMOTIVES USED DURING CONSTRUCTION

The principal Lynton & Barnstaple locomotives had the distinction of being the first in Britain to have the now universally accepted narrow-gauge features of outside frames and valve gear. Moreover the design was so successful that it was copied, with some modifications, for the Vale of Rheidol Railway in 1902 and a development of these locomotives is still in service today. However, we must first consider the heterogeneous collection of engines used during construction.

It is not known exactly how many locomotives were used by the contractor during the construction of the line. There were certainly three, probably four and possibly five. The first, and best known, of the 'certainties' was a diminutive 0—4—2 wing tank named *Excelsior*. She was built by W. G. Bagnall in 1888 for the opening of the Kerry Tramway in mid-Wales and carried the works number 970. When that line closed in April 1895 she was sold to Nuttall's, and was probably transferred straight to the Lynton & Barnstaple. On arrival, she carried a large spark-arresting chimney, but this was later exchanged for a straight stove-pipe. This remarkable little locomotive weighed only 2¾ tons in working order, developed a tractive effort of 1,290lb., and was fitted with Salter safety valves and double sheet-type smokebox doors. She later worked on the Portland stone tramways.

The second locomotive was an 0—4—0ST of the usual contractor's type, which was adorned with the name *Slave*. Unfortunately, only photographic evidence of this engine seems to have survived (see plate 3) and no further information can be given.

The last locomotive whose existence can be confirmed was another 0—4—0ST, built by Andrew Barclay of Kilmarnock in 1892. She was easily distinguished from *Slave* by her square saddle tank. There is no evidence that she ever carried a name, but she was known by the contractor's men and others as *Kilmarnock*, this no doubt being derived from the maker's plates. This locomotive, at least, was left on the railway's hands following the contractor's bankruptcy, for it is recorded in the director's minutes for 28 March 1900 'that the *Kilmarnock*, contractor's old engine, be sold for £120 or to the best advantage'.

It has proved more difficult to establish information about the fourth locomotive, except for a few details passed on by two L & BR employees whose association with the line began in the service of the contractor. At Parracombe, it was necessary to span the Heddon valley with a high embankment, and for this and other works in the area a 3 ft gauge locomotive named *Winnie* is said to have been used. Certainly broad gauge track was used in the area, for example in Martinhoe Cross cutting, but unfortunately this locomotive does not feature in any of the views of the construction which have come to light. *Winnie* is reported to have been delivered from Barnstaple to Parracombe along the main road under her own steam and assisted by four horses. Information on just how this was managed is vague and conflicting.

Information on the possible fifth locomotive is even more scanty, but one source states that an engine named *Spondon* was used. This information is unconfirmed, but it is quite possible that *Spondon* was in use at the Lynton end of the line, or at some remote spot where it would escape general notice.

THE MANNING WARDLE 2—6—2T's UNDER INDEPENDENT OWNERSHIP

The company turned its attention to the problem of providing motive power as early as August 1896, and by the next month a satisfactory tender had been received. The directors then resolved 'that the tender of the Brush Electrical Engineering Company be accepted and that three locomotives be ordered at £880 each to include hand and vacuum brakes according to specification supplied, the engines to be completed by 31 March 1897. . . .' Unfortunately no reason why this contract broke down is forthcoming, but the low price is worth noting—less than the Festiniog Railway had paid for their first locomotives over thirty years before.

The final contract was approved during November of the same year. This was with Manning Wardle & Co. of Leeds, for three locomotives at £1,100 each. They were under construction when the Amalgamated Society of Engineers' strike of 1897-8 took place, bringing some of the draughtsmen back to the benches to keep things moving, but despite the strike, the locomotives were ready

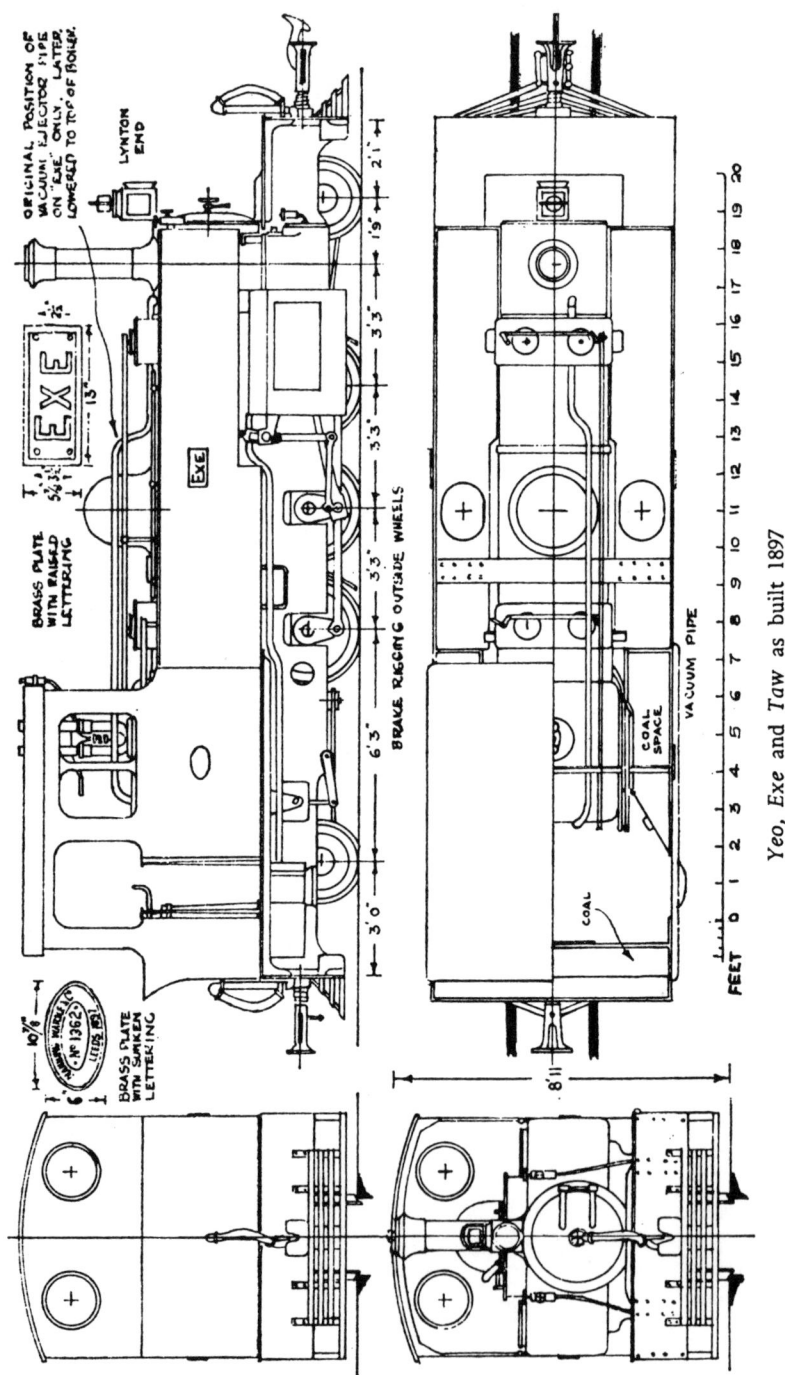

Yeo, Exe and Taw as built 1897

long before the contractor could relinquish possession of the works, and had to be stored by the manufacturers for some months. The board even considered whether it could not make a little on the side by hiring out one locomotive, but there is no indication that this was ever done.

The maker's numbers were 1361, 1362 and 1363, and the locomotives were named after the local rivers, *Yeo*, *Exe* and *Taw*. *Yeo* is said to have been delivered well before the other two, and to have been used in the final stages of construction, but *Taw* was on the line by March 1898. They were 2—6—2Ts with outside main frames and inside pony-truck frames. These locomotives were originally fitted with large cabs having two side windows. one in the cab itself, and the forward one ahead of the spectacle plate enclosing the safety valves. This formed a pocket in which steam collected and obscured the driver's vision, and so the cabs were altered between 1903 and 1913. The foremost side window was cut away, eliminating the troublesome front space, the roof moved back, and the rear bunker enclosed. These bunkers appear to have been used for almost anything but coal, the reason for this being probably the difficulty of swinging a shovel in the space available. Further coal-space had been provided pannier-fashion on either side of the firebox and this was increased very early on by the addition of steel sheeting. Joy's valve gear was hidden behind large motion covers, which had an inspection trap in the centre. It soon became the practice to run with these traps opened up, and after a few years they were removed altogether, and the openings were enlarged. The engines always ran with the chimney at the Lynton end, and so the chopper which the makers fitted to the rear coupling was removed, though according to an old driver, *Taw* was turned on one occasion, but only ran thus for a day or two. The chopper at the front end was usually hooked up when not in use. These three locomotives were always maintained as a class (unlike many other narrow gauge machines—for example, the Festiniog 0—4—0STT) and one of the few minor differences between them is readily apparent in photographs taken of the opening and very early days, when *Exe* ran with her ejector pipe raised well off the boiler. Another is the small capuchon which *Yeo's* and *Taw's* chimneys carried in the mid-1920s.

Few records of locomotive repairs survived, mainly due to the company's apparent willingness to leave all local matters entirely to Mr Jeune and the general manager. The only one to which the company's records refer took place in December 1910, when the

Avonside Engine Co. carried out extensive repairs on *Taw's* boiler, at a cost of £219.

The locomotives were always beautifully kept, and must have looked very smart in their original livery. Many of the early photographs show the polish worked into a fish-scale pattern, while the brasswork—chimney cap, dome and safety-valve covers, etc.—was invariably glittering. The basic colour was a deep green, often referred to as dark emerald or holly green. This was originally offset by a broad black line, with a narrower orange line inside. Later, however, the green was more simply relieved with a black border lined in orange.

The frames, cylinders, and other gear below the tank sides and running plate were painted in a reddish-brown shade, while the buffer beams and headlamps were vermilion, and both lined in the standard orange. The chimney, smokebox, cab roof, and tank-tops were black.

THE BALDWIN 2—4—2T 'LYN'

Although the company had hoped that three locomotives would suffice, it soon realised that this would leave no margin during the

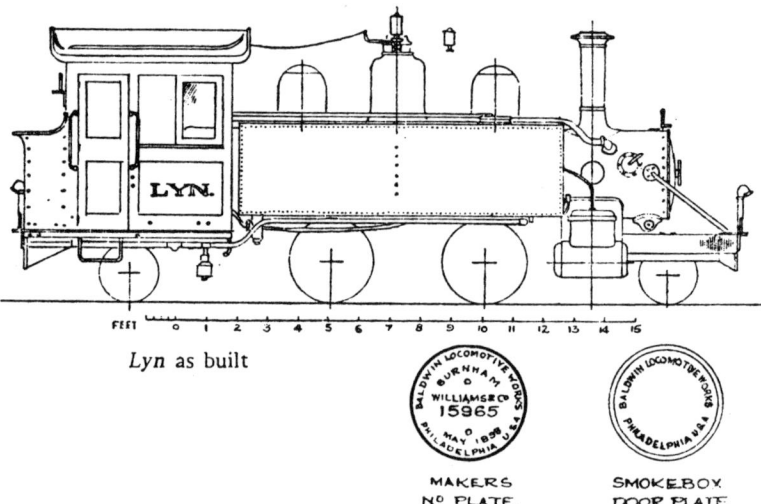

Lyn as built

MAKERS
Nº PLATE

SMOKEBOX
DOOR PLATE

summer season for emergencies, repairs or double-heading. Accordingly, the board decided to order a fourth engine from Manning Wardle & Co., or elsewhere, during February 1898. However, at this time all the suitable British builders had very full order books, and the company was therefore forced to take its order overseas, anticipating several other British companies, including such giants as the Great Northern and the Midland in so doing. The contract was given during April to the Baldwin Locomotive Works, of Philadelphia, who quickly designed and built a suitable machine.

The locomotive was shipped in parts to this country and erected at Pilton yard, where she was first steamed in July 1898. She was a typical Yankee 2—4—2T, with outside bar frames and equalised trucks of a special design. These were lavishly sprung, being suspended by transverse springs from an independent frame, which in turn was attached to a compensating beam whose opposite end carried the anchor at one end of the adjacent coupled-wheel spring. While this arrangement may have been essential on the more roughly laid tracks of Lyn's native land, it was but a refinement on the solid permanent way of the Lynton line.

The name *Lyn* appeared on the sides of her large wooden cab in elongated Roman lettering. Like the Manning Wardles, she was arranged for right-hand drive, with a 'pull-out' type regulator on top of the firebox. There was a maker's plate on the boiler side above the cylinders proclaiming that she was Baldwin's 15,965th locomotive, and that she had been built in May 1898. Another version of this plate adorned the front of the smokebox. In standard American practice, this would have been used to carry the locomotive's road number, but, being numberless, *Lyn's* had a blank centre. Another transatlantic innovation was the means of cleaning out smokebox ashes. Two small circular doors were provided in the smokebox side. These would be opened, a blow-off valve turned on, and a long rake pushed in. The driver then stirred up the ashes while the steam pressure blew them out below. This arrangement, which apparently worked well enough in America, did not find favour with the Lynton & Barnstaple enginemen. The steam dome was flanked by two rather smaller sand domes and was crowned with two Cole safety-valves and a 'siren' whistle, which was too tall to clear the loading gauge, and had to be off-set before the engine entered service. There is some doubt about her original livery, but former drivers, who in their younger days must have cleaned *Lyn* many times, state definitely and independently that she was painted black. She was lined out very simply with a single yellow line.

Like her stable companions, *Lyn* underwent various minor modifications during her early days. In fact, she required so much atten-

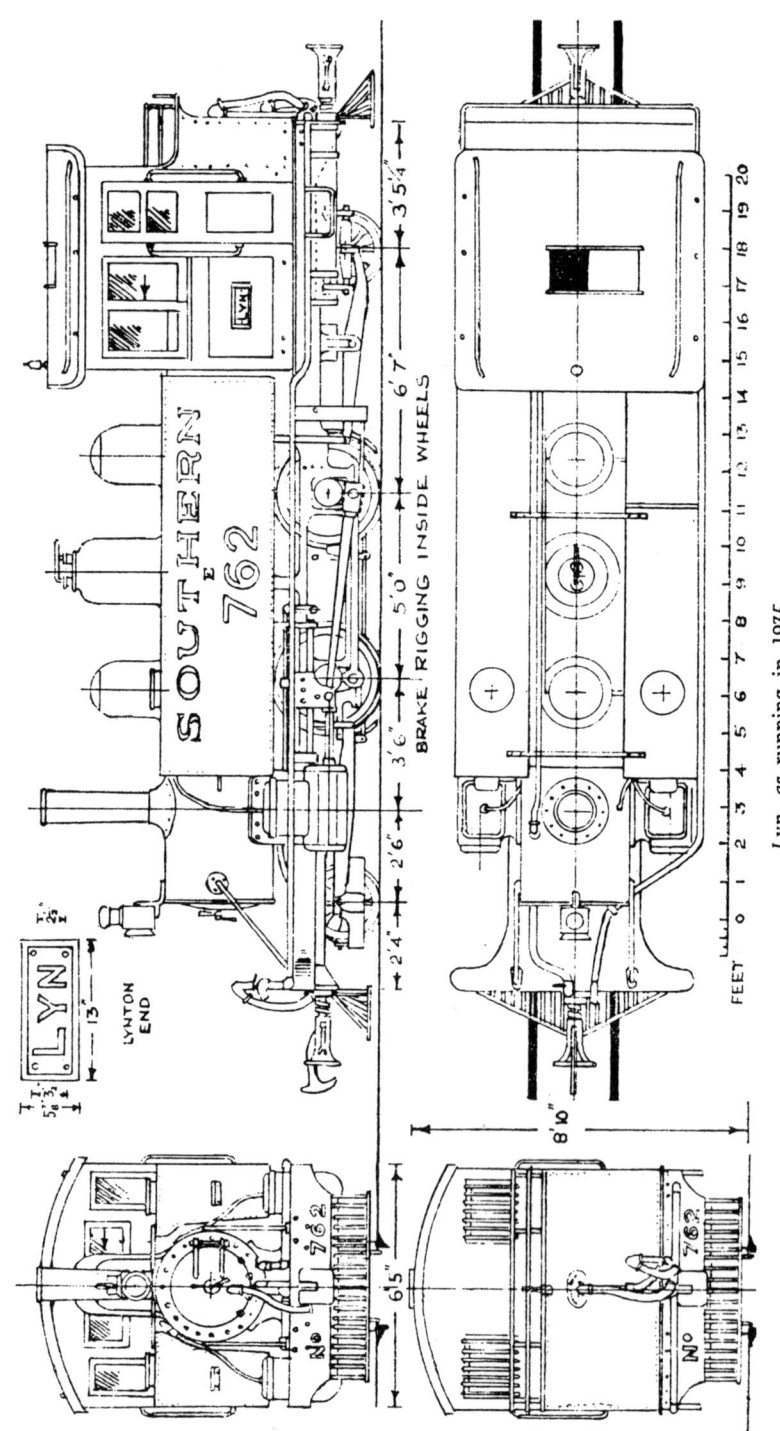

Lyn, as running in 1935

tion that, in 1903, Sir George Newnes complained that she had caused more trouble and expense than all the Manning Wardles put together. Within a year of her construction, the fitting of brass boiler-tubes was contemplated. An alteration carried out in the first few years was the fitting of a normal British-type smokebox door with locking handles, though the three lowest of the American rim locks were retained for some reason. At about the same time the names painted on the cab sides were covered by nameplates made up by the Pilton fitter from brass letters secured to a steel plate with copper rivets. Then, at about the time she was repainted in the standard Lynton & Barnstaple livery, several other modifications were made. Coal rails were fitted to the bunker, necessitating the removal of the rear lamp bracket first to the centre of the bunker rear panel, and later to a more visible position on top of the coal rails. Ramsbottom safety valves with a short release lever replaced the Cole pattern, and the 'siren' hooter was replaced by a bell whistle in the cab roof.

Although these early modifications changed her appearance considerably, they were structurally of a rather minor nature. However, while laid off for boiler inspection in 1907, the inspector's hammer penetrated one of her plates. Despite the high boiler pressure of 180 lb. per sq. in., the American boiler was very lightly constructed, and the wear which had taken place made patching-up impracticable. A new boiler was built by Avonside and the opportunity was taken to dispense with the unpopular ash-removing equipment.

Lyn ran in this handsome form throughout most of the company's independent life, but the Southern Railway lost little time in making detailed alterations. Her new ownership was first indicated by brass plates, which appeared on her cab-sides bearing the inscription 'Southern Railway E762'. To make room for these number-plates, the name-plates had to be moved to the centre of the side tanks. Also, just before grouping, she lost her stylish Baldwin copper-capped chimney for that form of utilitarian stovepipe so favoured during the Urie regime at Eastleigh. The next changes occurred in January 1929 when she returned from a complete overhaul at Eastleigh, resplendent in standard Southern livery. She differed from the Manning Wardles in that there was room on the side tank for her Southern number to be painted in 12in. letters. So the name-plates returned to the cab-sides. Unlike any of the other engines, except *Lew*, she carried her number also on the buffer beams. The final alteration was the fitting of steam heating equip-

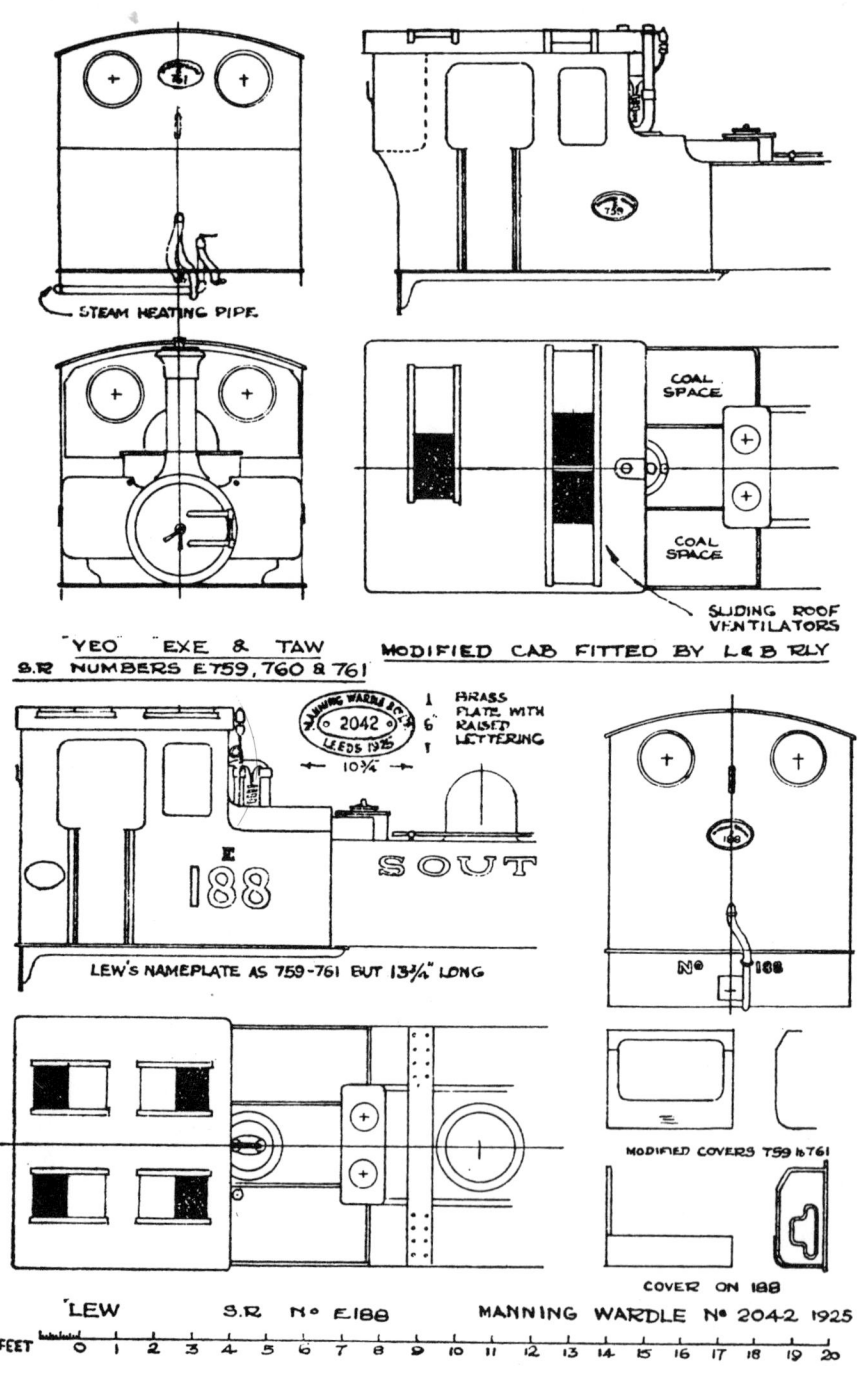

Cab details

ment in 1932, the train pipe running along the bottom left-hand side of the tank as on the British engines.

Lyn was always regarded by the drivers with rather less affection than the Manning Wardle locomotives. No doubt this was partly due to her Yankee origin, but she was fitted with inside Stephenson valve gear, which is far less accessible for oiling and maintenance than the 2—6—2T's outside Joy motion. Her lighter weight also made her prone to slipping. But in her favour it should be added that she possessed a greater degree of freedom on curves. with a rigid wheelbase of 5 ft as opposed to the six-coupled engines' 6 ft 6 in.

THE 2—6—2T's UNDER THE SOUTHERN RAILWAY

The condition in which the Lynton & Barnstaple Company maintained its locomotives has already been mentioned, and the Southern saw no immediate need for repainting. Indeed, at first, the only indication of change was the replacement of the makers' plates on the cab-side by oval brass plates carrying the Southern numbers —*Yeo* became E759, *Exe* E760, and *Taw* E761.

As part of its general improvement scheme, the big company decided to provide an additional locomotive. This arrived in 1925 from Manning Wardle & Co., and was very similar to the earlier machines. The rear coal bunker was omitted, and the cab was consequently straight instead of being swept back; the cab roof had four ventilators instead of three, and the safety valves had much shorter columns. The left-hand side bunker was extended in sheet steel as on the earlier engines, but the one on the right was fitted with coal rails: the motion was not covered, a cut-down version of the earlier engines' sheeting being fitted as a drip tray. Her maker's plates, in raised lettering, were carried on the bunker sides and bore the manufacturer's number, 2042. She was named *Lew*, after a central Devon watercourse, as the supply of local three-letter rivers had run out. Her number, E188, was out of series, but filled a gap in the South Western (E) group, left by one of the Adams '02' class 0—4—4Ts shipped to the Isle of Wight.

Lew set a new style in locomotive livery. The frames were now black, but all parts which had been green remained green, though a slightly different shade. The side-tanks were dominated by the word SOUTHERN in six-inch primrose lettering, relegating the name-plates to comparative insignificance, and the number appeared in standard twelve-inch numerals on the cab sides. The engine was neatly panelled in black with a thin white line on the inside. In time, all the other locomotives were repainted in this style, *Taw* and *Exe* apparently straight from L & BR livery, but *Yeo* ran for a few years in an intermediate style, similar to the later standard, but without the SOUTHERN and large number. The original 2—6—2Ts had one of their Southern number plates transferred to the back of the cab, but never had their numbers painted on the front buffer beam.

As has already been mentioned, *Lew* was the sole survivor. She was shipped to Brazil in 1936 and since then all trace has been lost.

COMPARATIVE DIMENSIONS

	Yeo, Exe Taw & Lew	*Lyn*
Weight, working order	27T 5 cwt	22T
Cylinders (2)	10½ in. x 16 in.	10 in. x 16 in.
Working pressure	160 lb/sq. in.	180 lb/sq. in.
Heating surface—total	383 sq. ft	379.2 sq. ft
Grate area	8.85 sq. ft	7.7 sq. ft
Tank capacity	550 galls.	664 galls. (800 U.S. galls.)
Coupled wheels (dia.)	2 ft 9 in.	2 ft 9 in.
Pony truck wheels (dia.)	2 ft 0 in.	1 ft 10 in.
Total wheelbase	17 ft 9 in.	17 ft 7 in.
Rigid wheelbase	6 ft 6 in.	5 ft 0 in.
Length over buffer beams	22 ft 4 in.	23 ft 6 in.
Length over drawgear	27 ft 0 in.	28 ft 0 in.
Width overall	6 ft 7in.	7 ft 2 in. (6 ft 7 in. over tanks and cab)
Height overall	8 ft 11 in.	8 ft 11 in.
Tractive effort @ 85% W.P.	7,269 lb.	7,418 lb.

BRATTON—BLACKMOOR

(30) *Near Bratton Fleming in July 1925*
(31) *South end of Blackmoor, c. 1922*

BLACKMOOR

(32) *Blackmoor—'Lyn' taking water*
(33) *'Yeo' near Blackmoor*

PARRACOMBE

(34) *Parracombe Bank*
(35) *Parracombe Halt*

Chapter 8

Rolling Stock

PASSENGER CARRIAGES

The company turned its attention to the provision of passenger rolling stock as early as August 1896, and while the directors had been content to leave the design of locomotives to the engineer, they had decided views on the form of coaches required, and the specifications for these were worked out at board level. The Bristol Wagon & Carriage Works Co. Ltd secured the contract in January 1897, undertaking to build 16 vehicles of six different types by 1 May 1897 for £7,300 less 10 per cent. Since all these carriages were of the same main dimensions and all had the same underframe, it is convenient to consider them generally in the first instance.

The carriages had wooden bodies on steel underframes in accordance with the best contemporary practice, but were unusual in that the floor was fixed direct to the underframe and not to the body structure. They ran on two massive plate-framed bogies, with the axle boxes and running gear *inside* the frames. Provision was made in the contract for the company to buy and supply roller-bearings if it wished, and that this was in fact done shows a progressive outlook. Unfortunately, however, these early roller-bearings soon tapered. In an attempt to secure even wear on these bearings, coaches were turned on the Pilton turntable, so that they did not always face the same way. But this did not prevent tapering and they had to be replaced with plain bearings as soon as renewals became due.

Lighting was originally by oil lamps, and unlike many other railway's coaches, those of the Lynton company were well lit, having one lamp in each compartment irrespective of class, and two in the saloons. The oil lamps were replaced by acetylene lighting before the First World War. Generators were carried in rectangular boxes at the ends of the coaches, one generator supplying gas to two coaches by means of a flexible tube connected about halfway up the end of the coaches. End steps and handrails gave the staff

Passenger rolling stock

access to the roofs for cleaning and filling the oil lamps, or maintaining the acetylene ones. The lamps could be removed if necessary and covers were provided for dropping into the lampholes on such occasions. These were fixed to the roofs by short lengths of chain. The principal dimensions were as follows:

Length overall	39 ft	6 in.
Length over buffer beams	35 ft	2 in.
Width over bodies	6 ft	0 in.
Width over steps	7 ft	4 in.
Total wheelbase	28 ft	10 in.
Bogie wheelbase	4 ft	4 in.
Wheel diameter	1 ft	6 in.
Height, rail to centre of roof	8 ft	7 in.
Height, solebar to cant rail	6 ft	4½ in.
Height, maximum internal	6 ft	6 in.

In common with all the rolling stock, the carriages had automatic vacuum brakes and Norwegian centre buffer-couplers. Side chains were fitted, but were all removed at an early date.

Only one further carriage was built, increasing the number of composite-brakes, which the company found to be a very useful type. This additional carriage was erected at Pilton in 1903, but just how much of the building was done by the company is open to doubt. The work is often attributed to Messrs Shapland & Petter, a local joinery firm, who probably built the wooden body. It is likely that the steel underframe was built in the Pilton Works, though the running gear may have come from the Bristol Wagon & Carriage Works, who supplied additional goods stock in the same year. Although generally similar to the older carriages, this one was slightly longer, being 36 ft 1½ in. over the body and 39 ft 10½ in. overall, with the bogies set at 25 ft centres.

First-class compartments were upholstered in blue cloth, or maroon leather in the smoking compartments. Arm rests were provided, allowing three-a-side in comfort. Third-class passengers, however, had to be content with four-a-side wooden seats, described as of the garden seat variety, and slatted with alternate strips of black and white wood. Fixed partitions were fitted between first-class compartments, between firsts and thirds, and to separate smoking and non-smoking thirds. Elsewhere, third-class compartments were divided by sliding partitions, which were bolted to the supporting framework of the luggage racks, or lowered between the seat backs, giving an open interior for summer use. Where these removable partitions were fitted, one large side window was provided to each pair of back-to-back seats. Luggage racks and curtains were provided in both classes, and mirrors in the first class.

Few external alterations were made over the years. The Southern sheeted over some of the toplights and carried out some repanelling in sheet steel. They also converted some of the first-class compartments to third, and fitted six vehicles with steam heating in 1932.

The passenger carriages were originally painted in a two-tone livery. The ends, lower panels and mouldings were a reddish-brown shade, while the upper panels were finished in varnished white. Classes were designated on the waist panel in gilt block letters shaded black, with the additional inscriptions 'Guard', 'Passengers Luggage' and 'Saloon' where appropriate. The roofs were painted white, and the lampholders, underframes and running gear black. The company's crest appeared several times on the lower panels, and consisted of a gilt circlet bearing the company's title enclosing two shields. One of these portrayed the Arms of the Borough of Barnstaple, and the other a deer which was intended to indicate the railway's association with Exmoor. Unfortunately, this colourful crest was not perpetuated, and when the coaches were repainted was superseded by the letters 'L&BR' on the waist panelling.

The passenger rolling stock list was as follows:

L&B No.	SR No.	Type	Original Class/Arr'ment	Seats 1st	Seats 3rd	Weight t.	Weight c.	Cost New		
1*	6991	Saloon Brake	1stO/1st/3/V	17	8	9	0	£463	2s	6d
2*	6992	,,	,,	17	8	9	0	,,		
3	2473	Saloon	1stO/1stS/1/1/3	28	8	8	16	£527	18s	6d
4	2474	,,	,,	28	8	8	16	,,		
5*	6364	Composite	3/3/1/1/3/3	12	32	8	16	£476	12s	6d
6*	6365	,,	,,	12	32	8	16	,,		
7*	2465	Third Obs.	3/3/3/30/3/3/3	—	50	8	16	£394	14s	6d
8*	2466	,,	,,	—	50	8	16	,,		
9*	2467	,,	,,	—	50	8	16	,,		
10*	2468	,,	,,	—	50	8	16	,,		
11	2469	Third	3/3/3/3/3/3	—	56	8	16	,,		
12	2470	,,	,,	—	56	8	16	,,		
13	2471	,,	,,	—	56	8	16	,,		
14	2472	,,	,,	—	56	8	16	,,		
15*	6993	Third Brake	3/3/3/3/V	—	40	9	0	£415	8s	6d
16*	4108	,,	,,	—	40	9	0	,,		
17*	6994	Compo. Brake	1C/3/3/1/3/V	9	24	9	0	—		

Notes: V = Van   C = Coupé   S = Saloon   O = Observation
   * = Fitted with acetylene generators

Towards the end of the independent company's existence some of the carriages were turned out in a one-colour livery. It has been impossible to confirm the exact shade used, but probably the upper panels were first painted to match the red-brown of the lower panels. There is also evidence to suggest that, in the early 'twenties, a dark green shade similar to that of the LSWR electric sets was used. It seems likely that for a few years three styles of painting were in existence at the same time, since the Southern painted the carriages in their standard green passenger livery, with black underframes and running gear and grey roofs, the interiors being finished in a light wood-grain shade.

Nos. 1 & 2. The directors were always keen to ensure that passengers should have as good a view as possible of the superb countryside, and these were two of the eight observation coaches which they provided. They had a large guard's and luggage compartment with duckets and a small end window, and contained the unusual provision of a dogs' box, having a small half-door, perforated for ventilation, in the lower panelling. The prospect of several dogs living in peaceful co-existence in this dark lurching compartment seems slight, and may account for the fact that in due course these boxes were removed. A conventional third-class compartment separated the van from the first saloon, which had seats for three across the end and three down each side. A glazed screen and door led from this into the observation platform, which had a central bench seat for six passengers, and was fitted with canvas blinds for lowering over the side openings in wet weather. As this defeated the object of the observation platform, the open sides were enclosed by about 1903 with four sliding lights, which also supplied the answer to requests which the company had received for spark guards.[7] Both coaches were fitted with steam heating by the Southern, and also escaped destruction after the sale. The remains of No. 1 became firewood, but No. 2 survives at Clannaborough Rectory as a garden summerhouse, the last L & B vehicle in recognisable form.

Nos. 3 & 4. These were a non-brake version of the previous type, the van portion being replaced by one third- and two first-class compartments. The saloon was larger than in Nos. 1 & 2, seating four down each side, and gave access to an open-sided first-class compartment having side doors and a solid end. The open compartment was later glazed in. In 1926 both these carriages were converted by replacing the first-class upholstery with wooden seats, in which form they seated 46 third-class passengers.

Nos. 5 & 6. These were composite coaches, having four third- and two first-class compartments, all divided by fixed partitions. They remained virtually unmodified until broken up.

Nos. 7-10. These four carriages were the company's only observation coaches for third-class passengers. The centre compartment was open above the waist, and was reached from the adjacent compartments through narrow half-glazed doors in the solid partitions. The seating capacity of 50 was made up of four in the observation compartment, seven in each of the adjoining compartments, and eight in each of the remaining four compartments, which were fitted with removable partitions. These carriages underwent only minor modifications, and although the canvas blinds were removed from the open-sided compartments, these were never glazed as the first-class ones were.

Nos. 11-14. These contained seven third-class compartments, two of which were divided off from the rest by a solid partition, and these were originally reserved for smokers, though smoking accommodation was later considerably increased. Removable partitions were fitted between the other compartments, making these extremely useful all-round vehicles. Two of them—Nos. 2471 and 2472—were fitted with steam heating in 1932-33, from which date they were usually to be found in winter trains.

Nos. 15 & 16. The last two of the original stock were a brake version of Nos. 11-14. The guard's compartment was slightly smaller than in the saloon brakes and did not include a dog box. It has been suggested that this luxury was reserved for first-class dogs! The passenger portion was divided by a fixed partition into one smoking and four non-smoking compartments, the other partitions being of the removable type. No. 16 ran in this form until scrapped, but No. 15 was converted into a composite at an early date, probably about 1903, seating 20 third- and nine first-class passengers. The rearrangement of the seating was achieved by repositioning certain of the partitions to form coupé compartments, increasing the space available for first-class compartments. The new arrangement was 3/1/1C/3C/3/V. Contrary to some earlier records the coach remained in this form until the closure, but with the legend '3rd' painted on the inside of all doors. It carried an acetylene generator and was fitted with steam heating in 1932-33, and after being sold for a mere £10 at the auction vegetated for 24 years on a short length of track near Snapper Halt, housing first evacuees and then hens, before taking up its new lease of life on the Festiniog Railway.

No. 17. Entering service in 1903, this coach contained smoking and non-smoking accommodation in both classes and was thus ideal for the operation of one-coach trains (*see* p 103). It is probable that it was especially built for this purpose as there were no other coaches with suitable accommodation until the conversion of No. 15. Although generally similar in appearance to the original coaches, there were other dimensional differences. The third-class compartments measured 5 ft between partitions and the first-class 5 ft 9 in. compared with the standard 4 ft 10 in. and 6 ft respectively. The van portion was 10 ft 8¾ in. long internally compared with 12 ft 1 in. in Nos. 1 & 2 and 9 ft 9 in. in Nos. 15 & 16. The first-class *coupé* served as an observation compartment, the end of the coach being glazed. This vehicle carried an acetylene generator and was fitted with steam heating in 1932-33.

The Lynton & Barnstaple's rolling stock was superior to anything seen on British narrow-gauge lines before or for many years after its introduction. The carriages were extremely well built, and were among the first in this country to be fitted with roller bearings. Although, as already mentioned, these early roller bearings did not stand up to wear, they were certainly helpful in reducing resistance, and the Festiniog Railway has decided to fit modern equivalents to its ex-L & B vehicle. The new Festiniog standard stock is being based on the design of the rebuilt L & BR No. 15—a high tribute to the straightforward excellence of the design—and the construction of what are virtually ten completely modernised Lynton & Barnstaple vehicles will prove most interesting.

GOODS STOCK

The original goods stock ordered in August 1897 comprised 14 four-wheeled and four bogie vehicles. One is tempted to think that the eight-wheeled type may have been an experiment, which, if so, was evidently satisfactory, since all further additions to the goods stock were of this type. The L & B livery was of light grey with white lettering and black ironwork and running gear. The Southern repainted them in its standard umber livery, again with white lettering, and it is interesting to note that some wagons retained their L & B numbers *after* being painted in Southern livery. Nevertheless, they had all been numbered in the Southern list by about 1927. Except where otherwise stated in the notes, all the goods stock was vacuum-fitted, and had a handbrake lever on one side only. Standard centre buffer-couplers were fitted, and the original stock also had side chains at the outset, though these were removed soon after the opening of the railway. Unfortunately official records of the goods rolling stock have not survived and other records show certain discrepancies. Nevertheless the authors believe the following notes to be as accurate as possible.

THE LYNTON & BARNSTAPLE RAILWAY
GOODS STOCK LIST

L&B No.	SR No.	Type	Builders	Date
1	28304			
2	28305			
8	28306			
9	28307	Open Goods	Bristol W & C Co.	1897
10	28308			
11	28309			
17	28310			
18	28311			
3	47036			
4	47037			
6	47038	Goods Van	Bristol W & C Co.	1897
7	47039			
15	47040			
16	47041			
5	56039	Brake Van	Bristol W & C Co.	1897
14	56040			
12	28301	Open Goods	Bristol W & C Co.	1897
13	28302			
19	28312	Open Goods		1900
20	28314	Platform Truck	Bristol W & C Co.	1902
21	28315			
22	28313	Open Goods	Bristol W & C Co.	1903
23	56041	Brake Van	L & B Rly	1909
24	28303	Open Goods	L & B Rly	1913
—	28316			
—	28317	Open Goods	J. & F. Howard	1927
—	28318			
—	28319			
—	47042			
—	47043	Goods Van	J. & F. Howard	1927
—	47044			
—	47045			

GOODS STOCK LIST

Outside Body Length	Dimensions Width	Tare Weight T. C. Q.	Capacity	Wheels	SR No.
10 ft 0 in.	5 ft 6½ in.	2 7 3 later 2 16 0	4 tons 4 tons	4 4	28304 28305 28306 28307 28308 28309 28310 28311
10 ft 5 in.	4 ft 11½ in.	2 11 3	4 tons	4	47036 47037 47038 47039 47040 47041
24 ft 5½ in.	5 ft 6 in.	5 18 2	8 tons	8	56039 56040
25 ft 10½ in.	5 ft 6 in.	5 5 2	8 tons	8	28301 28302
20 ft 7 in.	5 ft 0 in.	3 18 0	6 tons	8	28312
24 ft 7 in.	6 ft 3½ in.	4 0 0	8 tons	8	28314 28315
24 ft 7 in.	6 ft 3½ in.	5 5 0	8 tons	8	28313
24 ft 7 in.	5 ft 10½ in.	6 0 0	8 tons	8	56041
26 ft 1 in.	5 ft 7 in.	6 0 0	8 tons	8	28303
26 ft 3½ in.	6 ft 5¾ in.	6 1 0	8 tons	8	28316 28317 28318 28319
26 ft 5½ in.	6 ft 10¾ in.	6 6 0	8 tons	8	47042 47043 47044 47045

SERVICE VEHICLES

SR No.	Type	Builders	Date	
441S 442S	Travelling Crane	Chambers, Scott & Co.	?	Purchased secondhand from George Cohen & Sons 1926
	(Note similarity to ex-W.D. crane on the Festiniog Rly)			Lifting capacity: 15 ft radius 3 tons 11 ft 6 in. radius 4½ tons
441SM	Match Truck	Southern Rly Lancing	1927	Length 11 ft 3 in. Width 6 ft 8½ in. 8 wheel

NOTES ON THE GOODS STOCK

4-wheel Open. These were conventional narrow-gauge goods wagons, built on steel underframes. Originally they were fitted with a single top-hung side door each side, but these were replaced with pairs of side-hung doors at an early date, and tarpaulin rails were added by 1907. Originally, the sides masked the floors, but when the latter were renewed, the floorboards projected beneath the side planks. It was these wagons which one of the Lynton councillors likened to 'a child's wheelbarrow' when the Council was discussing steps to avert the closure of the railway.

4-wheel Vans. Based on the same underframe as the wagons, these vehicles had bodies of vertical matchboarding on internal framing, being free from exterior ironwork, and were fitted with a pair of sliding doors each side. They remained unmodified throughout their existence.

Nos. 12 & 13. These were the prototypes of the class, built on steel underframes with diamond-framed bogies, which were standard for the 8-wheel goods stock. They were originally fitted with top-hung side doors similar to those on the 4-wheel wagons, and by 1906 they had a pair of smaller top-hung doors each side, possibly as a result of the top planks distorting or breaking from the outward thrust of the load. Finally, pairs of side-hung doors were fitted as on the four-wheelers. The side doors were fitted to the left of centre when facing the vehicle.

No. 19. As soon as the railway was opened to traffic, it became

ROLLING STOCK 83

apparent that the directors had seriously underestimated their goods rolling stock requirements. However, with the company on the verge of bankruptcy, no further stock was added until 1900 when another bogie open appeared. This wagon is stated in all previous references to have been built by the Bristol W & C Works Co., but it was so unlike any of the earlier or subsequent 8-wheel stock built by that company for the L & B that this is doubtful. It bore such a striking resemblance to a vehicle used by the contractor that the authors consider it most likely that the railway company took it into its stock following the bankruptcy of the contractor. (It should be remembered that in 1900 the company was trying to dispose of the contractor's locomotive *Kilmarnock*.) The wagon was shorter, narrower and of smaller capacity than any of the others, and ran on a pair of plate-framed bogies of radically different design from the standard; it was originally fitted with a pillar handbrake, similar to that on the original bogie wagons of the Festiniog Railway, and was only piped for the vacuum brake. Unfortunately no further particulars of this interesting vehicle have come to light, but part of it appears in one of the plates.

Nos. 20 & 21. These were bogie flats used for carrying timber, pipes, rails and bulky loads such as hay, etc. They were built by the Bristol company in 1902 and were of slightly different dimensions from the original bogie wagons. Exceptionally they were fitted with full vacuum but no handbrakes. They had boarded ends and six detachable stanchions on each side.

No. 22. Delivered in 1903 by the Bristol company, and built to similar dimensions to those of the flats. The mainframe section of this wagon, together with the flats, was different from the originals, and it was fitted with a single side-hung door on each side, offset to the left of centre as in Nos. 12 & 13. It was piped only for the vacuum brake.

No. 24. The last wagon built for the line during independent days, and built by the company in 1913 at its Pilton works, which had become sufficiently well-equipped to undertake the construction of rolling stock. The vehicle followed the general standard design, and was similar in appearance to No. 22, but was fully fitted.

S.R. Nos. 28316-19. In view of the decreasing traffic and heavy operating loss which the Southern was already suffering, it seems curious that additional goods vehicles should have been ordered. These were four bogie wagons built in 1927 by J. & F. Howard Ltd of Bedford, and were very well-built vehicles indeed, readily distinguishable from the earlier wagons, as the side doors were located

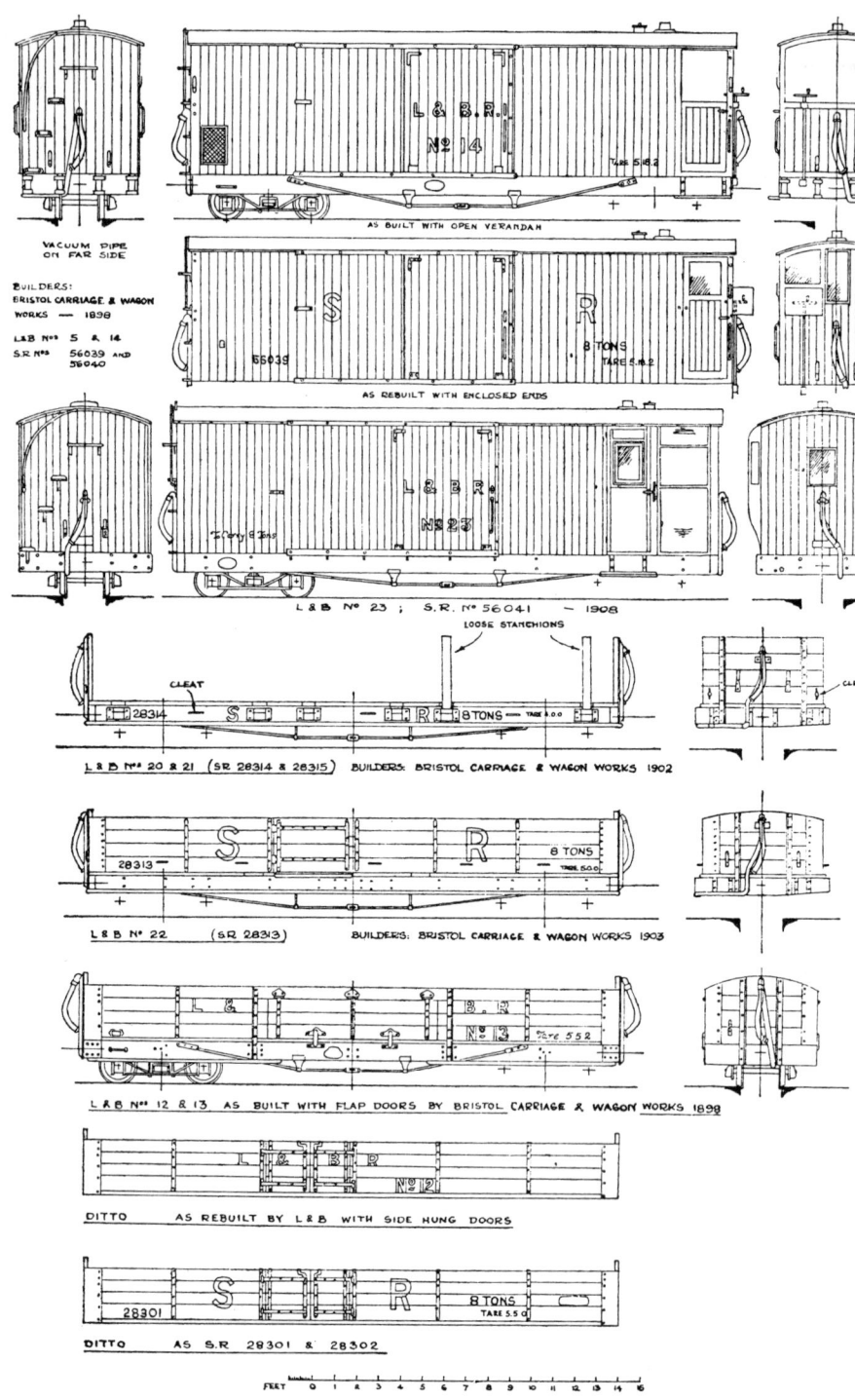

(Above and opposite) Goods rolling stock

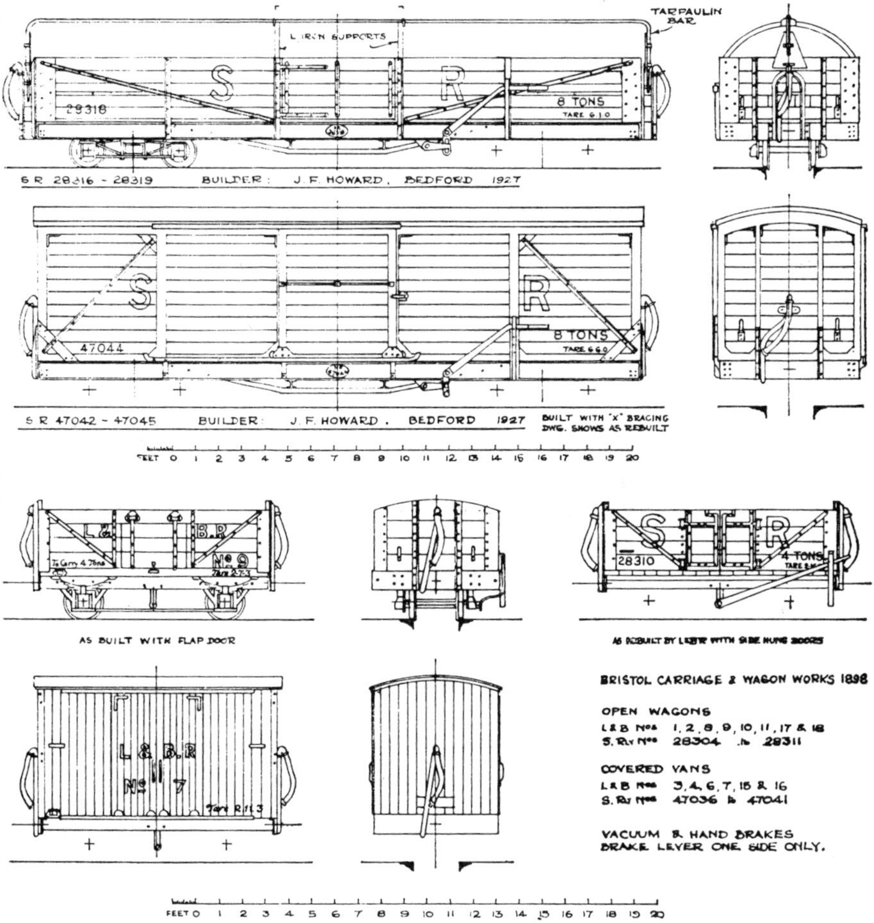

centrally, and they were fitted with a tarpaulin rail which had two hooped supports near its centre.

Nos. 5 & 14. These were the original goods brake vans, having an open guard's verandah reached by half-doors each side, and leading through a door in a half-glazed partition into the van proper. A pillar-type handbrake was fitted, with its column outside the verandah end. Vertical matchboarding on internal framing, similar to that of the four-wheel vans, was used and the van portion had a single sliding door each inside. At the end opposite the guard's verandah was a dog box, similar to that fitted in the saloon brakes, and this was removed at an early date. In about 1908 the verandahs were enclosed with end windows and glazed side doors, the handbrake wheel receiving a semi-circular sheet metal casing which protruded from the end of the van. They were fully vacuum-fitted and the underframes were similar to those on the original bogie wagons.

No. 23. In 1908 the company built this vehicle in its Pilton works, following the same general pattern as that of the original vans, but slightly wider and with more luxurious accommodation for the guard, who was provided with passenger-type side duckets. It was fully vacuum-fitted, but had the doubtful distinction of being the only timber-framed vehicle on the line.

S.R. Nos. 47042-5. These were the four bogie vans which J. & F. Howard Ltd built on similar underframes and running gear to those of the wagons which they supplied in the same year. They differed from the earlier bogie vans in that they had no guard's compartment and the bodies were of horizontal boarded construction with external wooden framing having double diagonal cross members. The latter were soon replaced by single angle-iron end braces. Single sliding side doors were fitted.

Nos. 441S, 442S & 441SM. The breakdown cranes were brought into use in 1927 and are thought to be ex-W.D. They were built by Chambers, Scott & Co., and were purchased by the Southern from Messrs George Cohen & Sons. Fitted with outrigger stabilisers they were designed to lift three tons at 15 ft radius; neither vacuum brake nor piping was fitted. There was little need for a breakdown crane on the L & B, where mishaps could normally be tackled with the aid of a couple of jacks, and in consequence one of the cranes, together with the match truck which the Southern built at its Lancing works, spent its life in idleness on the long headshunt at Pilton yard. The other was put to use in Lynton goods yard, where it stood on its own length of track ready to lift any heavy load that might be required of it. It is believed that after the sale, one of these cranes survived to see a further lease of life on the K & ES Railway, where it was mounted on a standard-gauge wagon.

CHAPTER 9

Operation of the Line

TIMETABLES

For the opening, a timetable comprising five trains each way on weekdays with one on Sundays was adopted. This necessitated one locomotive being shedded each night at Lynton, and was as follows:

LYNTON AND BARNSTAPLE RAILWAY.

LOCAL SERVICE between BARNSTAPLE AND LYNTON, and *vice versa.*

ALL TRAINS PARLIAMENTARY

DOWN.—Week Days.				a.m.		a.m.		a.m.		p.m.		p.m.			a.m.	
BARNSTAPLE (Town) ...	..	... dep.	6 35	...	8 46	...	11 30	...	3 45	...	5 24	...		7 30	...
Chelfham	...	...	...	,,	7 1	...	9 9	...	11 52	...	4 8	...	5 47	...		7 54	...
Bratton	...	...	...	,,	7 20	...	9 25	...	12 9	...	4 27	...	6 3	...	Sundays	8 15	...
Blackmoor	...	...	...	,,	7 45	...	9 50	...	12 31	...	4 49	...	6 28	...		8 40	...
Wooda Bay	..	...	...	,,	8 9	...	10 11	...	12 53	...	5 10	...	6 49	...		9 4	...
LYNTON ...	...	...	...	arr.	8 25	...	10 28	...	1 9	...	5 26	...	7 5	...		9 20	...

UP.—Week Days.				a.m.		a.m.		p.m.		p.m.		p.m.			p.m.	
LYNTON ..	...	...	... dep.	6 14	...	9 10	...	1 50	...	3 25	...	5 45	...		5 38	...
Wooda Bay	...	...	...	,,	6 33	...	9 28	...	2 8	...	3 43	...	6 3	...		5 57	...
Blackmoor	...	...	...	,,	6 58	...	9 53	...	2 31	...	4 6	...	6 28	...	Sundays	6 22	...
Bratton ..	...	...	...	,,	7 23	...	10 15	...	2 53	...	4 31	...	6 50	...		6 47	...
Chelfham	...	...	...	,,	7 40	...	10 29	...	3 8	...	4 46	...	7 5	...		7 4	...
BARNSTAPLE (Town) ...	...	... arr.	8 2	...	10 50	...	3 30	...	5 7	...	7 26	...		7 26	...

For a short time in the summer of 1898 there was a train which did not run the full length of the line. This left Lynton at 10.30 a.m. for Blackmoor, which was reached at 11.06 a.m., where after a quick turn round, it left for Lynton again at 11.15 a.m. No doubt this attempt to cater for the Ilfracombe coaching traffic was abortive, for it was not repeated afterwards. In these early years the first train down started from Pilton yard instead of from Barnstaple Town, presumably to save bringing out the crossing keeper for Braunton Road crossing and the signalman for Pilton yard box. The average journey times between stations at this time were Barnstaple—Chelfham, 22-23 mins down, 20-22 up; Chelfham—Bratton, 16-17 mins down, 15-18 up; Bratton—Blackmoor, 19-22 mins down, 19-23 up; Blackmoor—Wooda Bay, 19-21 mins down, 19-25 up; and Wooda Bay—Lynton, 16 mins down, 17-21 up.

From early 1899 onwards a pattern begins to emerge. The first train down—6.22 a.m.—connected with the overnight train from London bringing down newspapers and mail, and the first train up —leaving Lynton about 9.0 a.m.—connected with the principal London train, in later years to become the *Atlantic Coast Express*. On three days a week, the second train down left Barnstaple at about 10.0 a.m. and on the alternate days at about 11.30 a.m., when it provided a connection for day trippers from Ilfracombe, who had travelled to Barnstaple by the main London train already mentioned, at that time known as the *Alexandra*. The afternoon train which left Barnstaple at about 4.0 p.m. made a connection with the corresponding express from London, and on Fridays, for the market day traffic, an extra train was run shortly after 6.0 p.m. with a corresponding up train leaving Lynton about 8.0 p.m.

This pattern of three trains each way with an extra train on Fridays was broadly followed throughout the line's existence as the basic winter schedule, with the alternate day working of the second train being applied from November to April. During May, June and October it was usual to operate five trains each way on weekdays, made up of the basic winter service with both mid-morning trains run daily instead of on alternate days, and the 'Fridays only' late train run every day. From July to September the service was further augmented to give six trains a day by adding a further down train leaving Barnstaple about 2.30 p.m. This enabled travellers to make an after-lunch trip to Lynton and provided an extra train up about 4.0 p.m. to bridge the gap between 1.30 and 6.0 p.m. The second train down ran a little earlier, around 9.0 a.m., and its winter timing —about 10.45 a.m.—was taken by a seventh train (Tuesdays and Thursdays excepted) which returned from Lynton about 1.30 p.m. An eighth train ran down late on Thursday evenings—around 8.0 p.m.—to be stabled overnight at Lynton, in order to provide an early train up on Fridays only for market traffic. This pattern, with minor adjustments each year to maintain good connections at Barnstaple, continued through the early years of this century. The working timetable for June 1908 is on the next page. Special workings and holiday excursions were announced by handbills and, in early days at any rate, by advertisements in the local press.

WOODY BAY—LYNTON

(37) *Caffyns Halt*
(38) *Climbing through Barbrook Woods*
(39) *Running down from Dean Steep*

LYNTON—1

(40) & (41) *Entering Lynton, 1935*
(42) *'Yeo' at the buffer stops, 1935*

LYNTON—2

(43) *The first through train—19 March 1898*
(44) *Early days*

MANNING WARDLE LOCOMOTIVES

(45) *'Yeo' at Pilton in original livery*
(46) *'Exe' at Blackmoor, 1925*
(47) *'Lew' and wagon 28312 at Woody Bay, 1935*

DOWN	1 arr.	1 dep.	2 arr.	2 dep.	3 arr.	3 dep.	4 arr.	4 dep.	5 arr.	5 dep.	6 arr.	6 dep.
Pilton Yard		6E5	MO	8E45		10AE0		12.18	4.17	4L15	FO	5.33
Barnstaple T.	6.07	6.20	8.47	9.05	10.02	10.30	12.20	12.38		4.40		5.53
Chelfham	6.39	6.40	9.24	9.25	10.49	10.50	12.57	12.58	5.00X	5.01	5.52	6.09
Bratton	6.55	6.57	9.40X	9.42	11.04	11.05	1.12X	1.13	5.16	5.17	6.08	6.27
Blackmoor	7.15	7.18	9.59	10.00	11.22X	11.23	1.30	1.31	5.34	5.35	6.26	6.27
Woody Bay	7.36	7.38	10.18	10.19	11.41	11.42	1.49	1.50	5.53	5.55	6.45X	6.47
Lynton	7.53		10.34		11.57		2.04		6.10		7.02	

UP	1 arr.	1 dep.	2 arr	2 dep.	3 arr.	3 dep.	4 arr.	4 dep.	5 arr.	5 dep.	6 arr.	6 dep.
Lynton		8.50	MO	10.45		12.20		3.50		6.30	FO	7.10
Woody Bay	9.04	9.05	11.00	11.01	12.35	12.36	4.05	4.06	6.44	6.46	7.25	7.26
Blackmoor	9.22	9.23	11.19X	11.22	12.53	12.54	4.24	4.26	7.04	7.05	7.42	7.43
Bratton	9.39X	9.40	11.38	11.39	1.10	1.12	4.43	4.44	7.22	7.23	7.59	8.00
Chelfham	9.54	9.55	11.52	11.53	1.26	1.27	4.58X	5.00	7.37	7.38	8.14	8.15
Barnstaple T.	10.13	10E18	12.11	12E16	1.46	1L51	5.19	5H24	7.57	8E2	8.34	8E39
Pilton Yard	10A20		12.18		1.53		5J26		8.04		8.41	

Engine Workings
No. 1, up and down 1 and 3 (MO), 1 (MX)
No. 2, up and down 2 and 5 (MO), 3 and 5 (MX)
No. 3, up and down 4 (FX), 4 and 6 (FO)

Coach Workings
Train No. 1, Nos. 1 and 4. No. 6 (FO) down and up
Train No. 2, Nos. 3 and 5, No. 1 Sundays, down and up
Train No. 3, No. 2 Mondays only

Guards' Duties
No. 1, down and up 1 and 4
No. 2, down and up 3 and 5
No. 3, down and up No. 2 (MO) and No. 6 (FO)

NOTES

A   Mondays, engine of No. 1 up works No. 3 down without returning to Pilton Yard

E   Empty train

H   Empty train except Fridays

L   Light train

J   On Fridays, engine and train of No. 4 up works No. 6 down. No. 4 up no empty trucks on Fridays

MO   Mondays only

FO   Fridays only

Working timetable for June 1908

Subsequently, the Monday extra service was also operated on Fridays, thus giving two extra trains on market day. To meet summer demands, six trains a day were run, with an extra late one on Wednesdays, Fridays and Saturdays. When auction sales were held at Woody Bay or Blackmoor Gate during the winter, a short working left the former at 3.0 p.m. or the latter at 3.20 p.m. for Barnstaple. These sales were held about twice a month, usually on a Monday.

The war years naturally curtailed services and the basic three appear to have run—down at 6.20 a.m., 10.28 a.m., and 4.40 p.m., up at 8.10 a.m., 12.17 p.m. and 6.30 p.m., with the early morning extra service on Mondays and Fridays, and the late extra on Fridays only. During October 1915 an extra train ran down at 1.55 p.m. on Wednesdays and Saturdays, returning at 4.26 p.m., and by 1918 the extra early service on Mondays had been discontinued.

The service immediately after the war was also very meagre, the only addition to the 1918 service in June 1919 being an extra train which ran down at 12.5 p.m. (Fridays excepted), returning at 2.0 p.m. In June 1921 this pattern was repeated, and the following June, four trains a day were provided with an extra evening service on Fridays and Saturdays only. So to absorption by the Southern, with a mere shadow of the services provided in former days surviving.

The winter operating timetable for 1923 (opposite) affords an idea of the workings in early Southern days.

Over the years, inter-station times had been clipped a little and by this time were as follows:

Barnstaple—Chelfham, 19-20 mins down, 16-18 up; Chelfham—Bratton, 16-18 down, 14-15 up; Bratton Fleming—Blackmoor, 18-20 down, 17 up; Blackmoor—Woody Bay, 19-20 down, 18 up; and Woody Bay—Lynton, 14 down, 15-16 up.

The working timetable for the summer of 1924 is shown on the next page, and for the first time an optional goods working was included. This train left Pilton yard at 11.15 a.m. and arrived at Lynton at 1.12 p.m. Twenty-three minutes later it began its return journey, arriving back at Pilton yard at 3.19 p.m. For the following winter the second train ran daily instead of only on Fridays, and the fourth train down ran on Mondays, Wednesdays and Saturdays. Seven trains operated each weekday during the summer of 1928, and the following summer an additional late train ran down on Saturdays only. At this time one locomotive had to be stabled at Lynton during the summer and a 'lodging-out' turn was involved.

DOWN	1 arr.	1 dep.	2 arr.	2 dep.	3 arr.	3 dep.	4 arr.	4 dep.	4A arr.	4A dep.	5 arr.	5 dep.
										(N)		
Pilton Yard		6E5		8E29				10L20		12M55		4E15
Barnstaple T.	6.07	6.20	8.31	8.49			10.22	10.40	12.57	1.15	4.17	4.30
Snapper		6.30		8.59				10.50		1.25		4.40
Chelfham	6.38	6.39	9.07X	9.08			10.58	10.59	1.33X	1.34	4.48	4.49
Bratton F.	6.54	6.55	9.23	9.24			11.14	11.15	1.49	1.50	5.04X	5.05
Blackmoor	7.12	7.13	9.41	9.44			11.32X	11.33	2.07	2.08	5.22	5.23
Parracombe		7.25		9.56				11.45		2.20		5.35
Woody Bay	7.31	7.32	10.02	10.03			11.51	11.52	2.26	2.27	5.41	5.42
Lynton	7.46		10.17				12.06		2.41		5.56	

UP	1 arr.	1 dep.	2 arr.	2 dep.	3 arr.	3 dep.	4 arr.	4 dep.	4A arr.	4A dep.	5 arr.	5 dep.
Lynton		8.03		10.59		12.30		2.50		4.15		6.10
Woody Bay	8.17	8.18	11.12	11.13	12.44	12.45	3.04	3.05	4.30	4.31	6.24	6.25
Parracombe		8.23		11.18		12.50		3.10		4.36		6.30
Blackmoor	8.35	8.36	11.30X	11.32	1.02	1.03	3.22	3.23	4.48	4.49	6.42	6.43
Bratton F.	8.52	8.53	11.48	1 1.49	1.19	1.20	3.39	3.40	5.05X	5.06	6.59	7.00
Chelfham	9.06X	9.07	12.02	12.03	1.34X	1.35	3.53	3.54	5.19	5.20	7.13	7.14
Snapper		9.15		12.11		1.42		4.02		5.28		see below
Barnstaple T.	9.25	9L30	12.21	12PL26	1.53	1E58	4.12	4Q35	5.38	5E43	7.32	7E37
Pilton Yard	9.32		12.28		2.00		4.37		5.45		7.39	

NOTES

No. 2 down and up runs Mondays and Fridays to 29.10.23, Fridays only 5.11.23-25.4.24
No. 4 down runs MWSO to 31.10.23, MFO 2.11.23-28.4.24
No. 4 up runs MFO 2.11.23-28.4.24
No. 4A up runs MWSO to 31.10.23
E Empty train
L Light engine
M Light engine Mondays; empty train Wednesdays and Saturdays (to end October)
N Empty train Mondays; light engine Fridays (after end October)
P Light engine Mondays; empty train Fridays (to end October)
Q Light engine Mondays; on Fridays, the engine of the 2.50 p.m. up will, if required, pilot the 4.30 p.m. down

All trains stop at Parracombe when there are passengers to set down or take up; also (but during daylight only) at Snapper. Drivers & guards to be on look-out.

Working timetable for the winter of 1923

TIMETABLE EFFECTIVE FROM 14 JULY 1924

DOWN Type	Mixed arr.	Mixed dep.	Mixed arr.	Mixed dep.	Pass. arr.	Pass. dep.	Pass. arr.	Pass. dep.
Pilton Yard		6E05		6E50		8E25		10L30
B'staple T.	6E07	6.20	6E52	7.05	8E27	8.45	10L32	10.40
Pilton Yard		6.22		7.07		8.47		10.42
Snapper		6.30		7.15		8.55		10.50
Chelfham	6.37	6.39	7.22	7.24	9.02X	9.06	10.57	10.59
Bratton	6.52	6.53	7.37	7.38	9.19	9.21	11.12	11.13
Blackmoor	7.09	7.12	7.54	7.57	9.39X	9.42	11.29	11.31
Parracombe		7.24		8.09		9.54		11.43
Woody Bay	7.30	7.33	8.15X	8.19	10.00	10.02	11.49X	11.53
Caffyns		7.38		8.24		10.07		11.58
Lynton	7.45		8.31		10.14		12.06	

UP Type	Mixed arr.	Mixed dep.	Pass. arr.	Pass. dep.	Pass. arr.	Pass. dep.	Pass. arr.	Pass. dep.
Lynton		8.03		9.10		11.35		12.40
Caffyns		8.11		9.18		11.43		12.48
Woody Bay	8.17X	8.18	9.24	9.25	11.50X	11.52	12.54X	12.55
Parracombe		8.24		9.31		11.58		1.01
Blackmoor	8.34	8.35	9.41X	9.43	12.08X	12.09	1.11	1.12
Bratton	8.50	8.52	9.58	10.00	12.24	12.25	1.27	1.28
Chelfham	9.03X	9.04	10.11	10.12	12.36	12.37	1.39	1.40
Snapper		9.11		10.19		12.44		1.47
Pilton Yard		9.18		10.26		12.51		1.54
B'staple T.	9.20	9E25	10.28	10L45	12.53	12E58	1.56	2L01
Pilton Yard	9E27		10LA47		1E00		2L03	

A   Not run if required to assist 10.40 down
E   Empty train
L   Light engine

OPERATION OF THE LINE

FSO

Goods (R) arr. dep.	Pass. arr. dep.	Pass. arr. dep.	Pass. arr. dep.	Pass. arr. dep.
	2L25	3E40	4E20	6L35
	2L27 2.45	3E42 4.05	4E42 4.40	6L37 6.55
11.15	2.47	4.07	4.42	6.57
	2.55	4.15	4.50	7.05
11.30 11.34	3.02X 3.04	4.22 4.24	4.57 4.59	7.12X 7.16
11.47 11.50	3.17 3.18	4.37 4.38	5.12X 5.15	7.29X 7.30
12.06X 12.34	3.34 3.35	4.54X 4.57	5.31 5.33	7.46 7.48
	3.47	5.09	5.45	8.00
12.52X 1.03	3.53 3.55	5.15 5.17	5.51 5.53	8.06 8.08
	4.00	5.22	5.58	8.13
1.12	4.07	5.29	6.05	8.20

Goods (R) arr. dep.	Pass. arr. dep.	Pass. arr. dep.	FSO; Goods and empty Coaches arr. dep.	Pass. arr. dep.
1.35	4.25	6.15	6.40	8.35
	4.33	6.23		8.43
1.49 1.55	4.39 4.40	6.29 6.30	6.53	8.49 8.50
	4.46	6.36		8.56
2.11 2.25	4.56X 4.58	6.46 6.47	7.09 7.11	9.06 9.08
2.40 2.45	5.13X 5.14	7.02 7.03	7.26X 7.31	9.23 9.24
2.56X 3.05	5.25 5.26	7.14X 7.15	7.42	9.35 9.36
	5.33	7.22		9.43
3.19	5.40	7.29	7.56	9.50
——	5.42 5L47	7.31 7E36	——	9.52 9E57
	5L49	7E38	Will not run if engine req. to pilot 6.15 up	9E59

(R)   Runs when required
X   Crosses
FSO   Fridays and Saturdays only

The new winter pattern of four trains each way on weekdays, with the additional service at midday on Mondays, Wednesdays and Saturdays, continued till 1932, when the removal of the passing loop at Bratton Fleming necessitated some adjustments. For that summer seven trains ran each way on weekdays, and in the winter the pattern was resumed of four plus one on three days of the week. With the introduction of the summer timetable for 1932, an attempt was made to speed up schedules, and the 7.0 a.m. down was scheduled to pass Chelfham and Woody Bay, completing the journey in 81 minutes.

Services for 1933 were similar to those in the previous year, and for the summer of 1934 six trains a day were provided, with an extra evening service on Fridays and Saturdays. Following these patterns, we reach the final schedule which was as shown on p. 95.

The first train down passed Chelfham, and the second passed Snapper and Chelfham. In addition there was a Sunday service which varied its running from week to week. On 7 and 21 July and 15 and 29 September (this was the last train to run on this railway) it left Barnstaple at 11.50 a.m., arriving at Lynton at 1.17 p.m., returning from Lynton at 7.55 p.m. and arriving at Barnstaple at 9.22 p.m. On 14 and 28 July, 4, 11 and 25 August, and 1, 8 and 22 September it ran down one hour later and returned 90 minutes earlier, at 6.25 p.m.

The Southern National bus service had appeared in the timetable from the summer of 1931 onwards, and until 1962 the place names listed in the bus table printed in the Southern Region timetable were those of the principal railway stations.

It is perhaps worth taking a second look at the last timetable. The first and second down, first and third up could not have been of much use to travellers. Two were too early to be of any value and the other meant passengers forgoing lunch. Again, the holiday-maker in Lynton who felt like a day excursion found his last train home was the 4.25 p.m. from Barnstaple (except on Fridays and Saturdays).

From the foregoing description of the services provided, some of the difficulties in operating the line become apparent. Taking into account the overall journey times and the turn-round times at the termini, something like $3\frac{1}{2}$ to 4 hours was needed from an empty train leaving Pilton Yard until it had completed the round trip, not including time for remarshalling or locomotive purposes. To provide a higher-frequency service would have meant the employment of at least four locomotives and train crews but, as will be seen, the

LYNTON AND BARNSTAPLE BRANCH.

7th JULY to 29th SEPTEMBER only.

Distances M.	Distances C.	DOWN TRAINS. WEEK-DAYS. (To 28th September only.)	Pass. and Mail. arr. a.m.	Pass. and Mail. dep. a.m.	Pass. arr. a.m.	Pass. dep. a.m.	Pass. arr. a.m.	Pass. dep. a.m.	SXO Pass. arr. a.m.	SXO Pass. dep. a.m.	Pass. arr. p.m.	Pass. dep. p.m.	Pass. arr. p.m.	Pass. dep. p.m.
...	...	**Barnstaple** (Pilton Yd.)	...	...	...	6†45	...	9†55	...	...	...	1† 5	...	2†55
...	...	**Barnstaple Town**	...	5 33	6†47	7 0	9†57	10 15	...	*11 3*	1† 7	1 33	2†57	3 15
...	30	Barnstaple (Pilton Yd.)	5	35	7	2	10	17	*11*	*5*	1	35	3	17
2	55	Snapper Halt	5 44	5 44½	7	11	10 26	10 27	*11 14*	*11 14½*	1 44	1 45	3 26	3 27
4	55	Chelfham	...	...	7	19	10X35	10 36	*11 22½*	*11 23*	1X53	1 55	3 35	3 36
7	54	Bratton Fleming	6 5	6 5½	7 31	7 33	10 48	10 49	*11 35*	*11 35½*	2 7	2 8	3 48	3 50
11	62	Blackmoor	6 22½	6 23	7X50	7 51	11 6	11 7	*11 52½*	*11 54*	2 25	2 27	4X 7	4 11
14	34	Parracombe Halt	6 35	6 38	8 2	8 5	11 18	11 21	*12 5*	*12 8*	2 38	2 41	4 22	4 25
15	78	Woody Bay	6 45	6 45½	8 12	8 12½	11 28	11 30	*12 15*	*12 16*	2 48	2 49	4 32	4 34
17	36	Caffyns Halt	6 51½	6 52	8 18½	8 19	11 36	11 37	*12 22*	*12 23*	2 55	2 56	4 40	4 41
19	22	**Lynton**	7 0	...	8 27	...	11 45	...	*12 31*	...	3 4	...	4 49	...

DOWN TRAINS. WEEK-DAYS.	Pass. arr. p.m.	Pass. dep. p.m.	FSO *Pass.* arr. p.m.	FSO *Pass.* dep. p.m.		
Barnstaple (Pilton Yd.)	...	4† 0	...	...	...	...
Barnstaple Town	4† 2	4 25	...	*7 50*	...	...
Barnstaple (Pilton Yd.)	4	27	*7*	*52*	...	...
Snapper Halt	4 36	4 37	*8 1*	*8 1½*	...	...
Chelfham	4X45	4 46	*8 9½*	*8 10*	...	...
Bratton Fleming	4 58	4 59	*8 22*	*8 23*	...	...
Blackmoor	5 16	5 18	*8X40*	*8 43*	...	...
Parracombe Halt	5 29	5 32	*8 54*	*8 56½*	...	...
Woody Bay	5 39	5 40	*9 3½*	*9 4½*	...	...
Caffyns Halt	5 46	5 47	*9 10½*	*9 12*	...	...
Lynton	5 55	...	*9 20*	...	...	...

Distances M.	Distances C.	UP TRAINS. WEEK-DAYS. (To 28th Sept. only.)	Pass. arr. a.m.	Pass. dep. a.m.	Pass. arr. a.m.	Pass. dep. a.m.	Pass. A arr. p.m.	Pass. A dep. p.m.
...	...	Lynton	...	7 13	...	9 25	...	12 42
1	67	Caffyns Halt	...	...	9 33	9 33½	12 50	12 50½
3	25	Woody Bay	7 27	7 27½	9 40½	9 41½	12 57½	12 58½
4	69	Parracombe Halt	7 34½	7 37	9 48½	9 51	1 5½	1 8
7	41	Blackmoor	7X49	7 52	10 3	10 4	1 20	1 21
11	49	Bratton Fleming	8 8	8 8½	10 20	10 21	1 37	1 38
14	48	Chelfham	8 21½	8 22	10X34	10 36½	1X51	1 54
16	48	Snapper Halt	8 30½	8 31	10 44½	10 45	2 2	2 2½
18	73	Barnstaple (Pilton Yd.)	8	40	10	54	2A12	2 14
19	23	**Barnstaple Town**	8 42	9†15	10 56	11†25	2 16	2†39
...	...	**Barnstaple** (Pilton Yd.)	9†17	...	11†27	...	2†41	...

UP TRAINS. WEEK-DAYS.	Pass. arr. p.m.	Pass. dep. p.m.			Pass. arr. p.m.	Pass. dep. p.m.	Pass. arr. p.m.	Pass. dep. p.m.	FSO *Pass.* arr. p.m.	FSO *Pass.* dep. p.m.		
Lynton	...	3 30	...	...	...	6 7	...	8 4	...	*9 30*	...	...
Caffyns Halt	3 38	3 38½	...	...	6 15	6 15½	8 12	8 12½	*9 38*	*9 38½*	...	...
Woody Bay	3 45½	3 46½	...	...	6 22½	6 23	8 19½	8 20	*9 45½*	*9 46*	...	...
Parracombe Halt	3 53½	3 56	...	...	6 30	6 32½	8 27	8 29½	*9 53*	*9 55½*	...	...
Blackmoor	4X 8	4 9	...	...	6 44½	6 45	8 41½	8X42½	*10 7½*	*10 9*	...	...
Bratton Fleming	4 25	4 26	...	...	7 1	7 2	8 58½	8 59	*10 25*	*10 25½*	...	...
Chelfham	4X39	4 47	...	...	7 15	7 15½	9 12	9 12½	*10 38½*	*10 39*	...	...
Snapper Halt	4 55	4 56	...	...	7 23½	7 24	9 20½	9 21	*10 47*	*10 48*	...	...
Barnstaple (Pilton Yard)	5	5	...	...	7	33	9	30	*10*	*57*	...	...
Barnstaple Town	5 7	5†35	...	...	7 35	8† 0	9 32	9†38	*10 59*	*11† 5*	...	...
Barnstaple (Pilton Yard)	5†37	...	...	...	8† 2	...	9†40	...	*11† 7*	...	...	...

A—For exchange of enginemen only.

All services may be utilised for conveying vehicles containing goods traffic or empty goods wagons unless otherwise prohibited.
When goods vehicles are attached to the rear of the train, the last vehicle must be fitted with brake blocks operated by the vacuum brake.

Timing No. ...	320 — 7th and 21st July, 18th August, 15th and 29th September only. *Half-Day Excn. from Ilfracombe & Torr'gtn.* arr. a.m.	dep. a.m.	309 — 4th August and 1st September only. *Half-Day Excn. from Yeovil.* arr. p.m.	dep. p.m.	310 — 14th & 28th July, 11th & 25th August and 8th & 22nd September only. *Half-Day Excn. from Plymouth.* A arr. p.m.	dep. p.m.
DOWN TRAINS. SUNDAYS.						
Barnstaple (Pilton Y.)	...	*11†38*	...	*12†38*	...	*12†48*
Barnstaple Town	*11†40*	*11 50*	*12†40*	*12 50*	*12†50*	*1A 0*
Barnstaple (Pilton Y.)	*11*	*52*	*12*	*52*	*1*	*2*
Snapper Halt	...	...	...	...	...	...
Chelfham	*12*	*9*	*1*	*9*	*1*	*19*
Bratton Fleming	*12 21*	*12 22*	*1 21*	*1 22*	*1 31*	*1 32*
Blackmoor	*12 39*	*12 40*	*1 39*	*1 40*	*1 49*	*1 50*
Parracombe Halt	*12 52*	*12 55*	*1 52*	*1 55*	*2 2*	*2 5*
Woody Bay	*1 2*	*1 3*	*2 2*	*2 3*	*2 12*	*2 13*
Caffyns Halt	...	...	...	...	...	...
Lynton	*1 17*	...	*2 17*	...	*2 27*	...

Timing No. ...	310 — 14th & 28th July, 11th & 25th August and 8th & 22nd September only. *Return Half-Day Excn. to Plymouth.* arr. p.m.	dep. p.m.	309 — 4th August and 1st September only. *Return Half-Day Excn. to Yeovil.* arr. p.m.	dep. p.m.	320 — 7th and 21st July, 18th August, 15th and 29th September only. *Return Half-Day Excn. to Ilfracombe & Torr'gtn.* arr. p.m.	dep. p.m.
UP TRAINS. SUNDAYS.						
Lynton	...	*6 25*	...	*6 30*	...	*7 55*
Caffyns Halt	...	...	...	...	...	...
Woody Bay	*6 39*	*6 40*	*6 44*	*6 45*	*8 9*	*8 10*
Parracombe Halt	*6 47*	*6 50*	*6 52*	*6 55*	*8 17*	*8 20*
Blackmoor	*7 2*	*7 3*	*7 7*	*7 8*	*8 32*	*8 33*
Bratton Fleming	*7 19*	*7 20*	*7 24*	*7 25*	*8 49*	*8 50*
Chelfham	*7*	*33*	*7*	*38*	*9*	*8*
Snapper Halt	...	...	...	...	...	...
Barnstaple (Pilton Y.)	*7*	*50*	*7*	*55*	*9*	*20*
Barnstaple Town	*7 52*	*8† 0*	*7 57*	*8†12*	*9 22*	*9†40*
Barnstaple (Pilton Y.)	*8† 2*	...	*8†14*	...	*9†42*	...

A—Advertised departure time 12.50 p.m.

Final working time-table

volume of passenger traffic never justified this.

Moreover, where a train was operated in one direction to suit the requirements of the public, it was often counterbalanced by an inconveniently timed and lightly patronised working in the opposite direction. In particular, this applied to the provision of an early-morning up train and an evening down train. At times this difficulty was overcome by the institution of lodging turns, but since these were not a regular feature it is assumed that they were operationally inconvenient and possibly as costly as working poorly patronised trains. It is safe to assert that they were unpopular with the train crews.

These difficulties were embarrassingly obvious to the successive managements. The independent company, under the burden of its financial difficulties, just could not afford to steam a single engine more than was necessary to maintain a minimum service. At its best this was but a compromise between the desirable and what was practicable to the company. The Southern in improving the service discovered only too painfully the cost of doing so. Each did its best in the circumstances, but it is easy to appreciate the impossibility of providing an effective service to suit all demands.

STAFF

During the independent period, about 60 people were employed, and these were used, as near as can be ascertained, as follows:

BARNSTAPLE TOWN	1 Signalman and 1 man for transfer work at the siding (all station duties were undertaken by LSWR)	Total: 2
BRAUNTON ROAD CROSSING	1 Crossing Keeper, who filled in his time with odd jobs at Pilton yard	Total: 1
PILTON YARD	2 Signalmen	(Works)
	1 Goods Clerk	1 Foreman
	1 Goods Porter	1 Carriage and Wagon Repairer
(Office)	1 General Manager	1 Carpenter
	3 Clerks	1 Carriage Cleaner
(Running Staff)	3 Drivers (4 in summer)	2 Painters
	3 Firemen (4 in summer)	1 Blacksmith
	2 Passenger Guards	2 Apprentices
	1 Spare Guard	Total: 26 (28)
(Permanent Way)	1 Permanent Way Inspector	
	16-20 Platelayers	
	1 Signal and Telegraph Linesman	Total: 22

CHELFHAM	1 Porter Signalman
WOODY BAY	1 Stationmaster
	1 Porter (summer only)
BRATTON FLEMING	1 Stationmaster
BLACKMOOR	1 Stationmaster
	1 Porter
LYNTON	1 Stationmaster
	1 Warehouseman
	1 Porter (2 in summer)
	Total: 8 (10) Total for line: 59 (63)

In those days, of course, there were no rigid trade union rules prohibiting a man from doing several jobs. Staff would be moved around to meet summer needs, and it is possible that some of the platelayers worked as relief porters. Although there was no 44-hour week, staff relations were good and each winter all available employees were invited to a party thrown by the general manager in Pilton yard.

Nevertheless, one must agree that the stationmaster at Bratton Fleming who issued and collected tickets, collected, exchanged and re-issued tablets, signalled and sometimes crossed trains, and moved parcels and luggage, certainly earned his rather grand title. Equally hard-worked were the staff at Lynton, who in addition to normal duties, had to reheat the metal footwarmers which were used before the Southern introduced steam heating. These heaters would have to be collected from the compartments, the stoppers loosened, and the canisters placed before the fire, so that by the time the train was about to leave, the water would be hot again, the stoppers could be tightened, and the warmers placed in the compartments of the passengers who wanted them. If time was short, there was only one thing to do—draw hot water from the engine!

EQUIPMENT

The track was well drained, and comprised 30 ft long flat-bottom rails weighing 40 lb. per yard, and originally spiked direct to 4 ft 6 in. long sleepers placed at 2 ft 6 in. centres, with clips and bolts used to secure the rails at their ends to the first sleeper. The joints were fish-plated, and the points were clipped and bolted. but there were no check rails or tie rods used, even on the sharpest curves. Tyer's automatic tablet instruments were used throughout, those at Barnstaple Town and Pilton Bridge being located in the signal boxes, while elsewhere they were installed in the booking offices. The signalling equipment was supplied by Evans, O'Donnell & Co., and all points and signals, which were interlocked, were controlled from the signal boxes at Barnstaple Town and Pilton Bridge, at other stations from ground frames suitably placed, and at the Lynton end of Pilton yard and Braunton Road Crossing by ground frames, these latter controlling points only for entry into the yard and the wharf siding respectively. The signalling arrangements at the intermediate stations were standardised to provide a home and a starter signal in each direction, no distant signals being provided anywhere on the line. Originally at Lynton, the home signal comprised a single post with one signal above the other, the upper controlling entry to the main platform and the lower one the bay platform. The up starter signals consisted of two separate posts placed at the end of and to the left of the bay line and the main platform. Subsequently both up and down signals were replaced by bracket posts carrying two signals each. At Barnstaple Town an up home was provided, midway round the curve to the wharf, and a down starter at the end of the platform. At one stage in the line's existence this latter signal was moved to the right-hand side of the runround loop, but subsequently was returned to the end of the platform.

This signal is of particular interest in that at various times it appears to have been slotted to Pilton Bridge Box and to the LSWR Box at Barnstaple Town. The former presumably permitted early morning trains to be run without the manning of Barnstaple Town Box (as empty trains were propelled from Pilton yard back to Barnstaple Town) and the latter allowed the mainline to hold a train to effect a connection. The signals controlled from Pilton Bridge Box comprised an up home, situated just beyond the Lynton end of the yard, an up starter, situated on the passing loop before it joined its partner and the yard line to run over Pilton Road Crossing, and a down home which was situated some yards before Braunton Road Crossing. This was originally a single arm, but later consisted of a post bearing two home arms, the upper for entry into Pilton yard and the lower for the main line. It is suspected that this was the original down home post at Lynton and that it was transferred when the bracket signals were installed there. Other movements at Pilton yard were controlled with flags and lamps by the signalman.

The exit at the Lynton end was, however, in regular use for a few years in early days, when the first train down each day started from Pilton yard and not from Barnstaple Town. A goods working which ran direct from Pilton yard was provided in Southern days, but it was rarely used. In these days there also were occasions when an empty up working in summertime on Fridays and Saturdays only ran direct into the yard from Lynton. For these rare occasions, the Pilton yard signalman operated the ground frame at the Lynton end of the yard which was locked by the box from which he also controlled movements at other times.

GOODS TRAFFIC

The transfer siding at Town Station was only used for the transfer of complete wagon loads, consisting mainly of coal, manure (particularly in the spring), grain, bricks, timber, and telegraph poles.

Parcels traffic was conveyed by passenger train and transferred across the Town Station platform. Smalls and general goods, originating off the system, were conveyed to Barnstaple Junction, or Barnstaple (GWR), and transferred to Pilton yard goods shed by road. This cartage was carried out by Chaplins (taken over by Pickfords just before the line closed) and included beer, soap, confectionery, hardware, flour and groceries. Any goods from local Barnstaple traders would also be delivered to Pilton yard. Most of this general traffic was carried in the eight-ton covered and brake vans, for easy unloading. Lynton goods were loaded first, furthest from the doors, and articles for intermediate stations progressively towards the centre, with those for Chelfham right opposite the doorway. The number of articles for each station was shown on the wagon label as a check. The volume of traffic from the Junction would vary, being eight to ten tons per day during the summer, rising to twelve tons and more over Whitsun and August holiday times. Most of it, amassed during the day, was moved down by the first train. Overnight traffic from London was moved over from the Junction in time for the down train which left about 11 a.m., and occasionally a little was moved down by the late afternoon train about 4.30 p.m. In summer an eight-ton van was frequently attached to the 4.30 p.m. for passengers' baggage. In addition, there would be wagon loads of produce, etc., from local traders.

In early days, some of the coal arrived at Pilton Wharf by small coasters which usually carried cargoes of 200-300 tons for a merchant at Lynton, and were loaded direct to rail at the wharf. In pre-Southern days Welsh steam coal also arrived at the wharf, and was moved by horse and cart (shame!) to Pilton yard. In some years the total coal traffic for Lynton exceeded 1,000 tons, but for the other stations it was usually about 150 tons for Woody Bay, 500 tons for Blackmoor, and about 30 tons for Bratton Fleming. Before the First World War there was mention in the company's Minute Book of the possibility of heavy iron ore traffic which was intended for shipment through Fremington, but this did not materialise.

Traffic in the up direction was small by comparison, comprising principally wool, potatoes, hides, sheep skins, and rabbits for the London market. In addition the traffic in pitprops became quite heavy during the First World War.

At Lynton the cartage was carried out by Mr Tom Jones under contract, and during the last few years by Mr E. Porter. The journey from Lynton down to Lynmouth involved a 1 in 4 hill. on which a horse-drawn cart would take one ton at a time, skids being fitted under the wheels to maintain control.

THE PATTERN OF TRAFFIC

The following statistics show the trends of traffic:

YEAR	PASSENGERS				GOODS (TONS)			
	First	Third	Total	Seasons	Mineral	General	Train Miles	Livestock Receipts
1901	6,836	69,780	76,616	1	1,463	3,588	56,060	£6
1902	6,910	75,953	82,863	1	2,810	5,095	58,062	£6
1903	7,550	83,363	90,913	2	3,013	5,227	57,636	—
1904	6,869	82,231	89,100	2	2,763	4,402	56,301	—
1905	7,426	84,717	92,143	4	2,115	4,341	54,544	—
1906	7,535	87,126	94,661	1	3,022	4,692	55,243	—
1907	7,735	93,127	100,862	2	2,420	4,577	56,413	—
1908	6,989	91,745	98,734	2	2,860	4,636	56,708	—
1909	6,534	96,766	103,300	6	3,372	5,002	57,681	—
1910	6,333	96,806	103,139	7	3,089	4,929	57,583	—
1911	6,289	93,474	99,763	7	2,829	4,804	57,133	—
1912	5,461	93,906	99,367	6	3,216	4,856	57,688	£6
1913	5,621	103,406	109,027	7	3,396	4,960	—	—
	*3,571	*81,311	*84,882	* 7	*1,579	*2,802	—	
1919	*4,024(?)	*95,800(?)	*99,824	* 9	* 312†	*4,013(?)	50,590	—
1921	*1,873	*76,173	*78,046	*13	* 264†	*2,431	54,050	—
1922	*1,687	*71,628	*73,315	*20	* 560†	*2,331	54,296	—
	2,269	91,553	93,822	20	3,150	4,097	54,296	—

* Originating on system (balance transferred from LSWR or GWR)

† Of these totals, 213 (1919), 221 (1921) and 420 (1922) are coal, presumably over the wharf; probably one, one and two coaster-cargoes

(?) Suspected to be totals, not only traffic originating on system, although shown as such in official statistics

LYN

(48) *Following erection—Pilton, 1898*
(49) *At Lynton, July 1925*
(50) *With 'Yeo' at Pilton, 1935*

PASSENGER ROLLING STOCK

(51) *Saloon Brake No. 2—1898*
(52) *3rd No. 2466—1935*
(53) *3rd Brake, No. 4108—1935*

OPERATION OF THE LINE

There do not seem to be any other figures available, and as can be seen, some of these are suspect. Moreover, the practice of altering the details required for these official figures from time to time makes direct comparison difficult. However, certain points can be deduced.

(a) First-class travel reached its peak in 1907, and then dropped slowly. After the war it seems to have been small with less than 600 from the main line.

(b) About 20,000 third-class passengers came from the main line. Probably most of them were holidaymakers in the mid-July—August period.

(c) The height of passenger travel was in 1913, and the fall thereafter can be largely accounted for by the drop in first-class passengers. This may have been because they were the first to have motor cars, or because it became fashionable to take holidays abroad.

(d) Goods traffic seems to have been steady at about 7-8,000 tons, with a slight decrease in generals in latter years.

(e) The amount of livestock carried was very slight. Sheep were put in open wagons with nets over the tops to prevent them from jumping out. Cows were carried in vans, and two cows, nose to tail, just fitted side by side into a four-ton van. A brick was then jammed between the doors, and the handles tightly secured together with rope, thus providing ventilation for the animals.

(f) From a closer examination of the figures for 1913 and 1922, where it is possible to extract traffic transferred from the main line, the following pattern emerges:

On the passenger side, there is the 20,000-odd each year which did not originate on the system and can be considered as being made up principally of holidaymakers and day trippers from Ilfracombe, Bideford and other places. Unfortunately. we do not know whether these figures are based on journeys made or tickets issued (in which case return tickets might count as one). However, it is reasonable to think that they are based on passenger journeys, so it would seem also reasonable to allow for a further 20,000 journeys (probably 10,000 returns) which originated on the system, leaving between 55,000 and 70,000 journeys made by local inhabitants. This is a little over 1,000 a week, or 500 each way. Allowing for, say, 100 extra passengers to Barnstaple market on a Friday, this leaves 400, or about 70 passengers a day each way in addition to the market travellers. Thus in the winter months, apart from Fridays, two-coach trains were quite adequate. Similarly, it can be seen that the 40,000 single journeys (or at least most of them) were accomplished in the short summer season of at most eight weeks. Further, the majority of these would have been, in all probability, during the fortnight over August Bank Holiday, and would have amounted to at least 1,000 extra passengers on a Saturday, with a further 2,000 return trips each week.

On the freight side, we see that the total mineral traffic remained fairly static at around the 3,200-ton mark, but that the proportion transferred from the main line increased from about 1,500 tons to 2,500 tons. In the first place, this probably represents a reduction in the number of coasters handled at the wharf from five or six to about two. Bearing in mind the considerable reduction in coastwise shipping over the period of the First World War, this seems quite probable; alternatively, it may reflect a change in source of fuel from South Wales to other parts of the country. There is also a slump of 500 tons in local traffic carried, and of 400 tons in traffic transferred. The former, and possibly the latter, may be due to the emergence of the motor lorry after the war. Even so, there is a pattern of about 50 tons per week of generals originating on the system, plus 35 to 40 tons transferred from Barnstaple Junction, Barnstaple GWR, or over the transfer siding. Of this total, 50 or 60 would have been conveyed in the eight-ton vans, the remaining 30 tons or so representing full wagons of generals transferred at the transfer siding each week. (It should be remembered that some generals are very light and would not permit a wagon to carry its maximum load.) Presuming that most of the mineral traffic was coal arriving during the nine winter months (September to June), say 40 weeks, we have between 40 and 60 tons a week transferred at the Town siding, or roughly 12 tons a day.

It now only remains to complete the 1921 and 1922 picture by breaking down the generals figures. These were flour, bran and offals, 145 and 167 tons; grain, 246 and 201 tons; manure, 107 and 201 tons; potatoes, 64 and 110 tons; vegetables other than potatoes, 29 and 233 tons (these were mainly up traffic).

Cartage for 1922 cost £597, of which £138 was recovered from passenger traffic and £459 attributed to goods.

After 1922 no further figures are available, the statistics lying hidden in the results of the Southern, but it can be seen that during the few years when the line made a modest profit, it was quite busy, and the nature of the traffic was such that considerable fluctuations, season by season, had to be met.

THE OPERATING TECHNIQUE

In latter years, the first train down each day consisted of an eight-ton covered van, with generals loaded at Pilton yard goods shed the previous afternoon, any full wagons from Pilton, full wagons from the transfer siding, and a compo. brake coach.[8] It seems probable that this train was marshalled by the last train up at night and left in a siding at Pilton ready to be propelled up to Barnstaple Town station for the first train down. This connected with the overnight mail and paper train from Waterloo and on arrival at Lynton would be broken down, and a fresh train of two coaches with any full or empty wagons (rarely available so early in the day) would then be put in service for the first up train. The compo. brake would remain at Lynton for cleaning and would return on the last train up. Likewise, the two coaches used on the first train up would reach Lynton on the last train down and remain overnight in the bay platform. During the last years, when the first train was very early, two coaches were used on the first train down, which later formed the up train, but this departure from the earlier practice may have been adopted because of the quicker turnround allowed, 13 minutes compared with 17 minutes.

Goods wagons were usually marshalled between the engine and the coaches (except for Bratton Fleming down traffic which was coupled at the rear of the train), but with the introduction of steam-heating to some of the coaches, it became the practice in winter to marshal all wagons at the rear. Before this, on arrival at Lynton the engine was detached, run over the crossover to the yard, and collected outgoing wagons, which would then be hauled up the runround loop. The engine would then back these wagons on to the coaches, and propel them, plus the wagons it had brought in, over the crossover into the yard. The incoming wagons would be shunted to the places required, and the engine would then draw forward the outgoing wagons and coaches on to the platform road, ready for passengers to embark for departure.

So we have a pattern of goods wagons being worked down on the first train, and most empty and any full wagons being brought up on the last train. In addition, it was usual for an eight-ton van to be attached to the mid-morning down train (about 10.30 a.m.). This train also connected with the excursion train from Ilfracombe and in the summer was frequently double-headed (as was the corresponding up train which left Lynton about 6.0 p.m.). On arrival at

Lynton, the train (if double-headed) would halt at the Lynton home signal and the pilot engine would be detached and run forward on to the bay platform. The train engine would then draw the coaches forward on to the main platform, and the pilot engine would immediately depart for Pilton light. The eight-ton van would be placed in the goods shed for unloading, being returned to Pilton empty or under load later the same, or maybe the next, day. With the preponderance of traffic down, it was not customary to leave empty wagons down the line unless earmarked for specific work, but rather to collect them and return them to Pilton yard for future use.

The maximum load for one engine was four coaches or about 50 tons gross. If traffic exceeded this it was usual to resort to double-

Lynton and Barnstaple Railway. DOWN.

Engine Driver's Report. _Satun_ day, _Aug 10_ 1901 _6 20_ Train.

STATIONS	Service Time				Actual Time				Vehicles Attached					Vehicles Detached		REMARKS
	Arrival		Departure		Arrival		Departure		Coaches	Brake Van	Goods Loaded		Empty	Goods Trucks		
	H.	M.	H.	M.	H.	M.	H.	M.			Goods 8 W.	Goods 4 W.		8 W.	4 W.	
Barnstaple					6	34			2		1	2				
Chelfham					6	52		53								
Bratton					7	9	7	10								
Blackmoor					..	28	..	32								
Wooda Bay					..	49	..	50								
Lynton					8	4										
TOTAL																

Time finished duty

H A Fennell Driver's Signature.

A driver's report of 1901

heading when the maximum load for two engines was nine coaches, rather than to provide an extra train. To meet a temporary heavy load a down train might detach a coach at Bratton Fleming or Blackmoor. This would enable an extra wagon or so to be picked up at Lynton on the return run, and after passing the most adverse grades the coach could be reattached for the descent to Barnstaple. Again, if traffic was heavy a second engine would be used from Barnstaple to Blackmoor Gate, after which one engine could handle five coaches. Similarly, when required, the engine from the 4.25 p.m. down would pilot the 6.7 p.m. up as far as Blackmoor Gate, whence it doubled back smartly to work the 8.4 p.m. up.

When coal arrived at the wharf by coaster, all available open wagons were assembled at Pilton yard and shunted to the wharf as required. As soon as loaded, they were attached to the next available train to Lynton, where the coal merchant employed a special gang to discharge the wagons quickly, for return to Barnstaple.

Empty trains from Pilton yard to Barnstaple Town station were usually run in reverse, so saving running round at both ends. If transfer traffic was very heavy, it was sometimes dealt with by an engine from Pilton yard bringing down empties and taking back full wagons, which would then be attached to a convenient train before it left the yard. It seems that at no time was the line operated on the 'one-engine-in-steam' principle, although sometimes the timetable would have permitted this. Even on Sundays it was not always possible, for sometimes a relief train was required and all seventeen coaches were in use.

Base for proposed water tank near Bratton Fleming station

CHAPTER 10

Anecdotes and Conclusions

TALES OF THE LINE

There are many tales about the line. One concerns an occasion in the early days, when a party of American tourists chartered a special train comprising a saloon brake and an engine, from which to see the district. In typical Edwardian style they had furnished themselves with a luncheon hamper on a lavish scale, and on arrival at Lynton in the evening, presented the train crew with the ample remains of their rations. The engine was to be stabled overnight at Lynton in readiness to convey the managing director to Barnstaple early on the following morning. Several bottles of wine, partially finished, were among the remnants of the hamper, and the process of disposing of the engine for the night was a somewhat hilarious and bibulous affair. In the cold light of dawn, the footplate men awoke to find themselves in a quarry some distance from the station, whither they repaired with haste and sinking hearts to find their worst fears confirmed—a dead fire and the boiler barely warm! Some sleepers from the PW gangs' store nearby soon found their way into the firebox, and soon the crew's spirits rose with the pressure-gauge needle. Sufficient steam was raised in time to carry the unsuspecting VIP to Barnstaple. Nevertheless, Blackmoor was reached before enough pressure was available to create a vacuum, and the descent from Woody Bay to Parracombe was controlled by the handbrake. Perhaps we should explain that it was common practice when shunting stock to open the valve of the vacuum cylinder. This valve was situated on top of the cylinder with a length of wire attached, and in this way the vacuum brakes were released. The crew had had to resort to this dodge in order to move the coach!

Another tale concerns *Lyn's* original footplate fittings, which included screw-down valves to the water-gauge glasses, in place of the more usual lever handles which could be shut down by a 90-degree turn. On one occasion a gauge-glass burst while working a down train, filling the cab with steam, before the driver managed to shut down the valve. Having done this, he was just in time to haul his young fireman back on the footplate, for the latter, terrified by the roar of escaping steam, was on the point of baling out at one of the line's several precipitous locations. The driver delivered an appropriate reprimand and the young fireman learned a timely lesson!

Animals were a constant hazard on this line. Chickens would fly squawking from beneath the very wheels above Snapper, and trains might stop in the neighbourhood of one of the hillside farmsteads while the engine crew cleared the line of young cattle. Sheep often fled before the train near Woody Bay, seeking an avenue for escape. A small terrier was once seen being pursued through the level crossings at Barnstaple, yelping defiance over its shoulder at the steaming, hissing monster behind. Some animals seemed unmoved by the approach of the trains and even regarded the latter as trespassers on their tranquillity. One somnolent pig could only be persuaded to move by a ringing blow across the rump from a fireman's shovel. Early one morning the down mail came to a halt when the crew spotted a red deer entangled in the wires of the lineside fence, at the foot of an embankment. Driver and fireman descended, the latter with his clasp knife open and no doubt with the smell of venison steak in his nostrils. Whether the deer sensed their motive or not, their approach spurred it to greater efforts, it gave a terrific heave to free itself and leapt away into the dawn's half-light.

A young fireman from Exmouth Junction was preparing *Lyn* for duty one day, and left it in full fore gear while he went into the works. When he returned, *Lyn* was way down the headshunt, having collected some wagons on the way, and was busy trying to push these, and presumably the crane as well, through the stop block!

There was also the driver who, after shunting at Chelfham, left his train there and did not miss it until he reached Pilton.

Moving from the tales of engine crews, there is the story of the stationmaster at Woody Bay who enjoyed both his pint and his gardening. But the general manager had a summer hut in the grounds of Woody Bay Hotel, at which he spent most week-ends. Therefore, before imbibing, or slipping off to his garden on a Friday, the stationmaster would ring up Pilton office to enquire whether 'mumble-mumble' was on the train down. All the office staff knew whom he meant by 'mumble-mumble' and would tip him off accordingly. But one day this weekly conversation went something like this:

Stationmaster: Is 'mumble-mumble' on the train?
Voice at Pilton: No, not today; this is 'mumble-mumble' speaking!

Another story concerns a Lynton man who used to arrange for an inspection trolley to be left near Woody Bay station during the week. On Sunday, with his wife and small daughter, he would walk to Woody Bay, place the trolley on the track and come roaring back down to Lynton with only a piece of wood as a brake.

One driver used to claim that he was paid Royalty Money, presumably referring to two of Queen Victoria's daughters, Princess Christian and Princess Victoria, who travelled on the line while visiting the area about 1905.

CONCLUSIONS

The fate of the Lynton & Barnstaple Railway was perhaps inevitable, and due to changing times and customs. The line's inherent limitations may have been tolerated in the easier tempo of life at the turn of the century, but not in the motor age 30 years later.

If criticism is to be levelled at the Southern Railway it should not, in all fairness, be for closing the line as an uneconomic branch, but for viewing it as an ordinary branch at all. By the middle 'thirties all the British narrow-gauge lines which were to survive had abandoned the traditional concept of railway operation for something more suited to their particular traffic. But on the L & BR the service had changed only superficially since before the First World War, showing little flexibility in facing motor competition and a changed social order.

The Southern should be credited with trying to improve its possession, but some of the ways in which it sought to do so were ill-considered. For example, if a standby locomotive was really needed—and this seems doubtful when the independent company had operated successfully throughout with four—there were numerous ex-WD machines which were virtually new and which could have been purchased for a song in the early 'twenties. Again, it seems strange that eight new freight vehicles were needed in 1927 when goods traffic was at a lower level than before the First World War.

However, the final nail in the coffin of the line was the need to spend £2,000 per annum on track renewals over and above operating losses. It is this which will most surprise those familiar with the present-day privately-owned narrow-gauge lines, since the permanent way was in far better condition than that of the Festiniog Railway, for example, at the same time. One cannot help feeling that much of this expenditure arose by applying main-line thinking to a railway which should have had entirely different standards, and it is interesting to contemplate what might have been achieved had there been an all-out effort to adapt to local conditions in 1935.

The Vale of Rheidol has often been cited as an example of how the Southern should have treated the L & BR, namely by operating a summer-only service, and concentrating on the holiday and tourist traffic. In this, the essential difference between these two railways is easily overlooked. The Welsh line has a holiday town at one end and little at the other but scenic attractions which can easily be assimilated in the turn-round time of its trains. This shorter line moreover permits a very convenient half-day trip, an advantage also shared by the Talyllyn Railway and by the Festiniog in its present form. On the other hand, the L & BR had attractions at the Lynton end which would occupy the average excursionist for the whole day, as was shown by the heavy patronage of the 10.15 a.m down train, and the late afternoon or early evening up trains in the summer. The other trains throughout the day (except on Saturdays) carried little more than their winter complement of passengers. Virtually no tourists came for the unique journey through superb scenery, although had there been some imaginative local publicity, a few thousand more passengers might have been attracted. It must be remembered that narrow-gauge lines did not then have their present-day allure, and it is wishful thinking to suppose that the average excursionist would have made the trip solely for the experience of travelling by this unusual means. It seems therefore that the L & BR was already carrying a fair proportion of its potential summer traffic, and to abandon winter running would have meant losing the valuable parcels, mail and freight receipts without any economy resulting, as few staff cuts could have been made. The 'Vale of Rheidol Treatment' would have thus left the Lynton line in a worse position still.

Another solution to the line's problems would have been the introduction of a diesel railcar to handle most of the winter traffic, keeping steam stock for the busy holiday season. Although any attempt at accurate costing is handicapped by the lack of detailed statistics for the railway's later years, it is fortunate that records which the late Mr F. E. Box kept of passenger figures for the spring of 1935 have been passed down. These reveal that on three days in one week in early April, fourteen, seven and sixteen passengers alighted from the 9.25 a.m. up train at Barnstaple Town, while the 10.15 a.m. down train carried about the same number. Ridiculously few for a steam train with a crew of three, but not quite so hopeless if a one-man railcar had been available with, say, 24 seats and ample provision for mail, parcels and smalls. It is worth remembering that such vehicles were well established by the mid-'thirties in France and on the County Donegal Railways, where their judicious use had cut expenses dramatically. Such a railcar would have been able to maintain a regular parcels and mail service, and also to cope with steady, if not particularly heavy freight traffic by towing one or two wagons, with steam workings only on market days and during the peak holiday season.

Supported by parallel economies in operation—such as de-staffing intermediate stations—such measures would undoubtedly have reduced the annual deficit, but it is unlikely to have been eliminated. In the palmy pre-1914 days, when the railway managed to make a small profit, the number of passengers carried was about 100,000 a year. Twenty years later it was 32,000. What economies could possibly have offset this decline?

Thus, while such measures might possibly have succeeded in putting the L & BR back on its feet, they would probably have only postponed the inevitable for a few years, although had the line survived the Second World War, a brighter future might have awaited it in the world of preservation societies. Neither the independent company nor the Southern had made money on it. With the whole world in the throes of the depression, no speculator could have been expected to risk his capital where two proprietors had already suffered losses, and the Southern had little incentive to pour more capital into new measures, such as the railcar. Moreover, at that time, the Southern was investing very heavily in its large-scale electrification plans.

Thus, the unpalatable but inescapable conclusion is reached that anyone faced with the decision which the directors of the Southern Railway had to make, would almost certainly have been forced to follow the same course, and to run the last train on a Sunday evening, late in September, 1935.

Notes

1 (p 19)   The Minute Book states Bratton but the distance would refer to Blackmoor.

2 (p 19)   The contractor.

3 (p 35)   This official reference to transverse springing is curious, as the carriage springs were in fact longitudinal.

4 (p 54)   Some confusion has arisen down the years as to the identity of Collar Bridge. From the early photograph reproduced in Plate 10 it would appear that this was the name of the railway bridge over the River Yeo, but the staff always referred to the road bridge by this name because it marked exactly the start of the 'collar work' for the locomotives. It should be noted, however, that the minor road also crosses the river, and in some maps this location is named Collard Bridge. It seems most likely, therefore, that the staff adapted or corrupted this existing name to suit their own landmark. Similarly a cutting near Parracombe was named 'Blacklead Cutting' from the colour of the rock in which it was made.

5 (p 56)   On the right, near the second overbridge, could be seen the concrete base for a new water tank, which might be mistaken for a small platform. The purpose was to improve the water supply at Bratton Fleming station where the existing water tank would have been fed by gravity from the new supply tank instead of the laborious hand-pump. This project was in hand just before the railway was taken over by the Southern, who did not pursue the matter. The tank which had been acquired for the purpose was sold and was still in use on a neighbouring farm in recent years.

6 (p 57)   The stonework base of the water tank housed a hot-air engine which drove the water pump for supplying the tank.

7 (p 77)   At about this time the seating in this section was rearranged to four down each side.

8 (p 103)   Coaches 15 or 17 would be used for this purpose.

Appendices

1 : CHRONOLOGY

1854   North Devon Railway opened from Exeter to Barnstaple.
1873   Devon & Somerset Railway reached Barnstaple from Taunton.
1879   Bill launched for line from Lynton to connect with the Devon & Somerset Rly. at South Molton, but dropped.
1883   Barnstaple & Lynton Railway Bill published but dropped.
1884   Attempt made to promote a line from Lynton to Filleigh on the Barnstaple to Taunton line.
1885   Lynton Railway Act—Filleigh to Blackmoor Gate.
1886   Act secured for extension—Blackmoor Gate to Lynton.
1887   Act secured for branch—Blackmoor Gate to Combe Martin.
1890   Fresh Act secured, abandoning all but Lynton—Blackmoor section.
Lynton and Lynmouth funicular cliff railway and hydro-electric plant on E. Lyn River opened, both sponsored by Sir George Newnes.
1892   Bill promoted for tramway from Braunton to Blackmoor Gate to link with the Lynton and Blackmoor line, under the name of 'The Barnstaple & Lynton Electric Tramroad Co.'
Hollerday Hall built at Lynton for Sir George Newnes.
1894   25 September. Powers under 1890 Act lapsed. Public meeting held during the summer advocating narrow-gauge line from Barnstaple to Lynton. Immediately followed by promotion of a standard-gauge line from Filleigh to Lynton.
1895   19 March. House of Lords consider both schemes, approve the Lynton & Barnstaple Bill, and reject the Filleigh scheme.
May. Petition to Parliament presented at a public meeting in Lynton and received enthusiastically.
27 June. Lynton & Barnstaple Railway Bill received Royal Assent.
28 June. First board meeting, with Sir George Newnes as Chairman.
17 September. First sod cut by Lady Newnes on the site of Lynton station.
1896   5 March. Board accepted tender of £42,100 from Mr James Nuttall, adding £500 for completion of the line by 1 May 1897.
24 September. Draft agreement with LSWR for use of Barnstaple Town station approved for 30 years.
November. Tender for locomotives from Manning, Wardle & Co. of Leeds accepted.
1897   24 February. Board revealed that contractor had asked for an extension to 1 July 1897 to complete work, which had been refused.
18 October. Meeting between Board, Consulting Engineer and Mr Nuttall, junr., who promised completion by 1 January 1898.
1898   14 March. First train—*Taw* and one coach—ran through from Barnstaple to Lynton.
16 March. *Yeo* and two coaches conveyed a press party over the line.

APPENDICES 113

	Early May. Board of Trade Inspection carried out. 11 May. Official opening ceremony. 16 May. Line opened for regular traffic. June. Board agreed to change name of Bratton station to Bratton Fleming. July. *Lyn* entered service. The Minehead & Lynmouth Light Rly. scheme dropped after enquiry.
1899	20 February. Appeal Court announced decision in favour of company and against Mr Nuttall. 1 May. Mr Drewett became Traffic Manager. July. Parracombe Halt first appeared in timetable. November. Mr Drewett appointed Secretary and General Manager.
1900	Wagon No. 19 purchased.
1901	The name of Wooda Bay station changed to Woody Bay.
1902	Platform wagons Nos. 20 and 21 added to stock.
1903	April-August. First railway motor coach service run by Sir George Newnes between Ilfracombe and Blackmoor. Coach No. 17 and wagon No. 22 added to stock. Snapper Halt opened.
1907	*Lyn's* boiler condemned. Caffyns Halt opened.
1909	Goods brake van No. 23 built at Pilton yard.
1910	March. Mr W. J. Hart, platelayer, killed by train at Braunton Road Crossing. 9 June. Sir George Newnes died. Succeeded as Chairman by Sir Thomas Hewitt, K.C.
1913	26 March. Two men killed in accident near Chumhill. Open wagon No. 24 purchased. First dividend of ½ per cent.
1919	Sir Thomas Hewitt resigned as Chairman and succeeded by Col E. B. Jeune.
1921	Last dividend of ½ per cent (which had been maintained annually since 1913) declared.
1922	23 June. Terms of agreement reached for line to be absorbed by LSWR. Operating loss incurred.
1923	March. Final agreement reached, under powers provided by the Southern Railway Act 1923, for absorption. 1 July. The Lynton & Barnstaple Railway Co. ceased to exist as an independent entity.
1925	July. *Lew* entered service. 72,000 tickets issued.
1926	Two cranes purchased secondhand. Coaches Nos. 3 & 4 converted to all-third class.
1927	Match truck built at Lancing for the cranes. Operating loss of £5,900 incurred. Four open and four covered wagons purchased.
1931	Southern National bus timings included in timetable for the first time.
1932	Loop at Bratton Fleming removed and other economies made. The fitting of steam heating to the locomotives and six coaches commenced.
1933	Steam heating completed.
1934	32,000 tickets issued; some older employees moved to jobs elsewhere on the Southern Railway.

1935 11 April. Conference at the Castle, Barnstaple, to enlist support for the retention of the line, proved ineffective.
29 September. The last train ran.
8 November. Lifting of the track from Lynton to Milepost 15½ completed by the Southern Railway.
15 November. Sale of rolling stock, line and all equipment.
1936 Dismantling completed. *Lew* overhauled and shipped to Brazil.

2: LOCOMOTIVE MILEAGE

1925	Yeo	Exe	Taw	Lyn	Lew	Total
January	1,778	—	1,823	1,108	—	4,709
February	1,363	—	1,860	1,552	—	4,775
March	2,069	—	2,222	644	—	4,935
April	498	1,637	2,112	694	—	4,941
May*	—	1,355	1,774	189	—	3,318
June	2,336	2,101	365	764	—	5,566
July	2,256	2,912	—	1,814	10	6,992
August	2,683	3,101	1,547	1,843	362	9,536
September	3,021	2,525	1,116	—	1,362	8,024
October	1,917	1,699	831	—	974	5,421
November	1,392	1,938	785	—	495	4,610
December	1,684	2,349	264	—	304	4,601
TOTAL*	20,997	19,617	14,699	8,608	3,507	67,428
1926	18,822	15,920	12,606	3,080	15,059	65,487
1927	15,600	21,957	8,055	7,496	15,404	68,512

* One week's figures missing. May is therefore a three-week total only
Highest monthly total recorded, August 1927, 10,187 engine miles

3: LENGTH OF PLATFORMS, &c.

Location	Platforms Up	Platforms Down	Loop	Sidings, etc.
Barnstaple T.	—	326'	408'	Transfer = 368'; top of loop = 130'
Pilton Wharf (0.23.07)	—	—	—	Siding to catch point = 162'
Pilton Yard (0.32.19)	—	—	568'	Turntable line, table = 30'; lead-in = 105' Loco shed 1 = 58'; lead-in = 57' Workshop = 72'; loco shed 2 = 61'; lead-in = 124' Carriage shed 1 = 153'; lead-in = 125' Carriage shed 2 = 157'; lead-in = 105' Carriage shed 3 = 158'; lead-in = 104' Lead-in from loop to 2 & 3 = 63' Goods shed = 36'; lead-in = 224' Siding = 203'; lead-in to shed & siding = 102' Headshunt = 371'
Snapper (2.54.00)	—	132'	—	
Chelfham Via.	—	—	—	336' long
Chelfham (4.55.27)	221'	165'	455'	Sidings = 55'
Lancey Brook Viaduct (6.63.70-6.65.80)	—	—	—	140' long
Bratton Fleming (7.54.15)	204'	204'	416'	Long siding = 250'; short siding = 156'
Blackmoor (11.62.73)	216'	186'	428'	Up side, removed 1930 = 156' Down side, by platform = 252' by stables = 156' Headshunt (before lengthening, 1930) = 84'
Parracombe (14.33.63)	—	213'	—	
Woody Bay (15.77.97)	214'	214'	438'	Siding = 190'; headshunt 229'
Caffyns (17.35.74)	132'	—	—	
Lynton (19.23.08 at main platform stop block)	306' (Main)	360' 180' (Bay)		Goods shed = 40'; siding beyond = 113' Back siding = 260'; bay siding = 302' Loco shed and siding = 321'

4: DIMENSIONS, &c.

(Taken from Sale Catalogue)

PILTON YARD. The capacity of the road weighbridge was 5 tons. Amongst other items disposed of there were 7 steel side-tip wagon bodies and 9 old steel bodies. These were used for P.W. work and probably were originally left by the contractor. Also sold at Pilton were 2 platelayers' trolleys.

LYNTON SIGNAL CABIN. Boarded and glazed 9' x 8' x average 7' 6" with a seven-lever signal frame.

WOODY BAY SIGNAL CABIN. Boarded and glazed 6' x 5' x 7' with a seven-lever signal frame.

PARRACOMBE WATER TANK. Wrought iron 16' x 4' 6" x 3' 9".

BLACKMOOR WATER TANK. Cast iron 18' x 10' x 4' 6".

BRATTON FLEMING TANK. Cast iron 7' x 6' x 4' on four 6" x 12' columns.

CHELFHAM TANK. Cast iron 7' x 6' x 4' on 10' columns.

BARNSTAPLE TOWN. 10 cwt. jib crane with steel jib 7" x 7" x 16' plated timber posts, steel rail guys and ropes, and load gauge.

FREIGHT ROLLING STOCK

(54) *Wagon No. 12—1898*
(55) *Accident casualty wagon No. 10—1913*
(56) *Van No. 47044 on Pilton turntable, 1935*

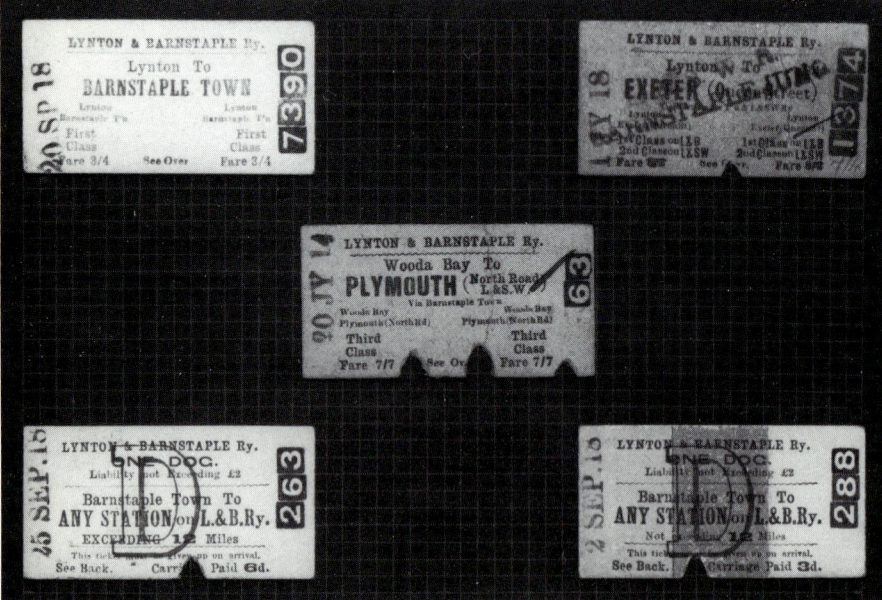

(57) *'Taw' passing Rolle Quay*
(58) *A selection of* L & BR *tickets*

5: STATION DRAWINGS

The five drawings on the following pages are included primarily for the benefit of modellers. The track layout of Lynton on page 119 was that used during the first years of the railway; note the double slip points at the approach to the platform and the cross-over laid in the reverse direction to that shown in the plan on page 60. As stated elsewhere, the plans in the text are taken from an LSWR survey of 1922.

The arrangement of the booking hall and office in the Woody Bay station plan is as latterly in use. It is believed that the original arrangement was as shown in the plans of Lynton and Blackmoor stations. The scullery was originally an open yard.

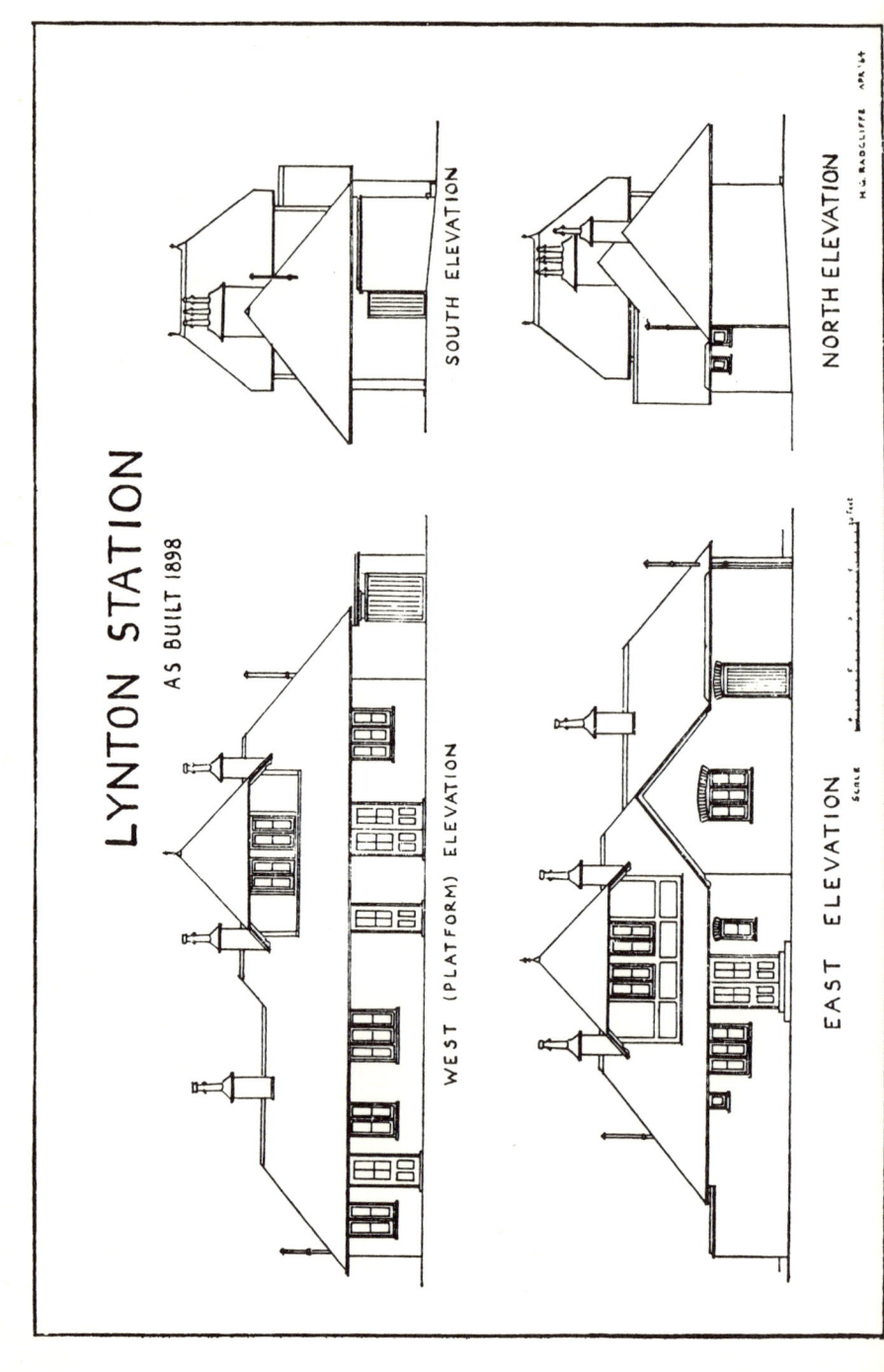

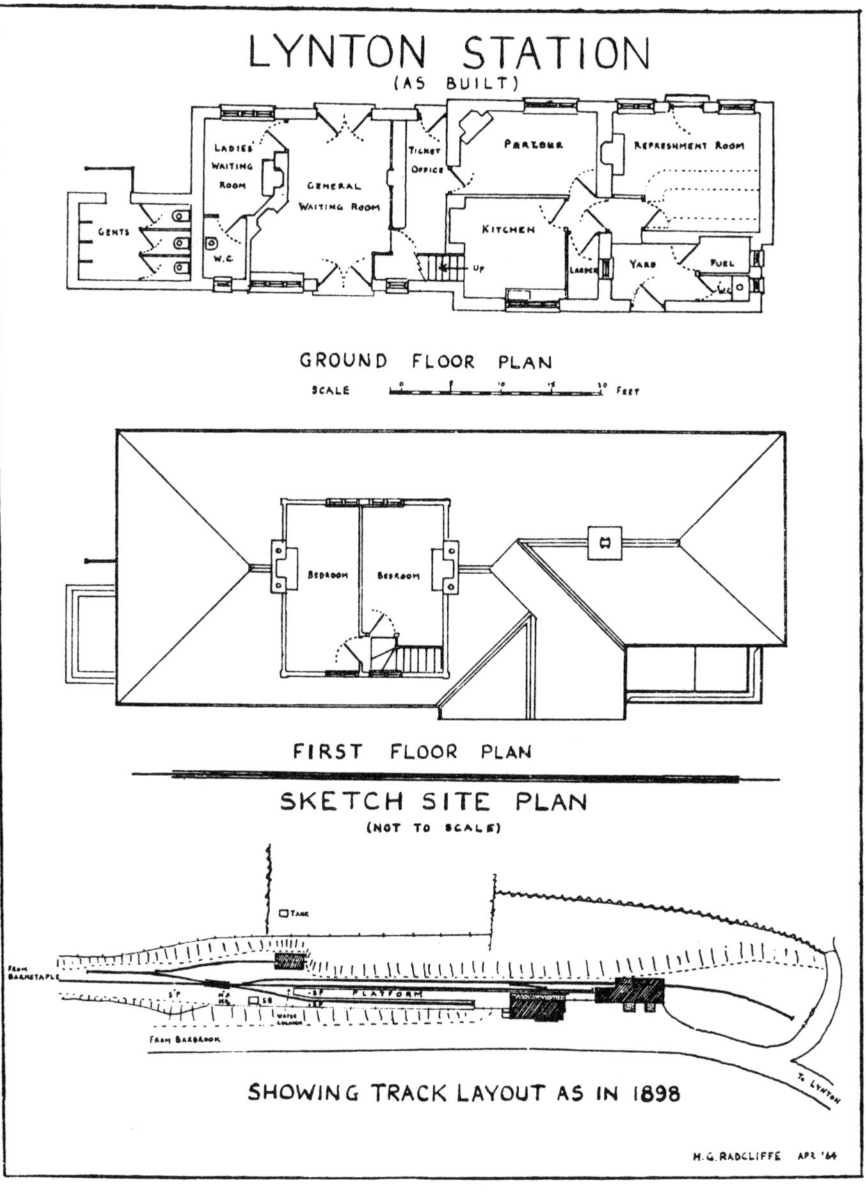
LYNTON STATION
(AS BUILT)
LADIES' WAITING ROOM
GENERAL WAITING ROOM
TICKET OFFICE
PARLOUR
REFRESHMENT ROOM
GENTS
W.C.
KITCHEN
UP
LARDER
YARD
FUEL
W.C
GROUND FLOOR PLAN
SCALE
0
5
10
15
20
FEET
BEDROOM
BEDROOM
FIRST FLOOR PLAN
SKETCH SITE PLAN
(NOT TO SCALE)
TANK
FROM BARNSTAPLE
S.P
PLATFORM
S.B
WATER COLUMN
FROM BARBROOK
TO LYNTON
SHOWING TRACK LAYOUT AS IN 1898
H.G. RADCLIFFE APR '64

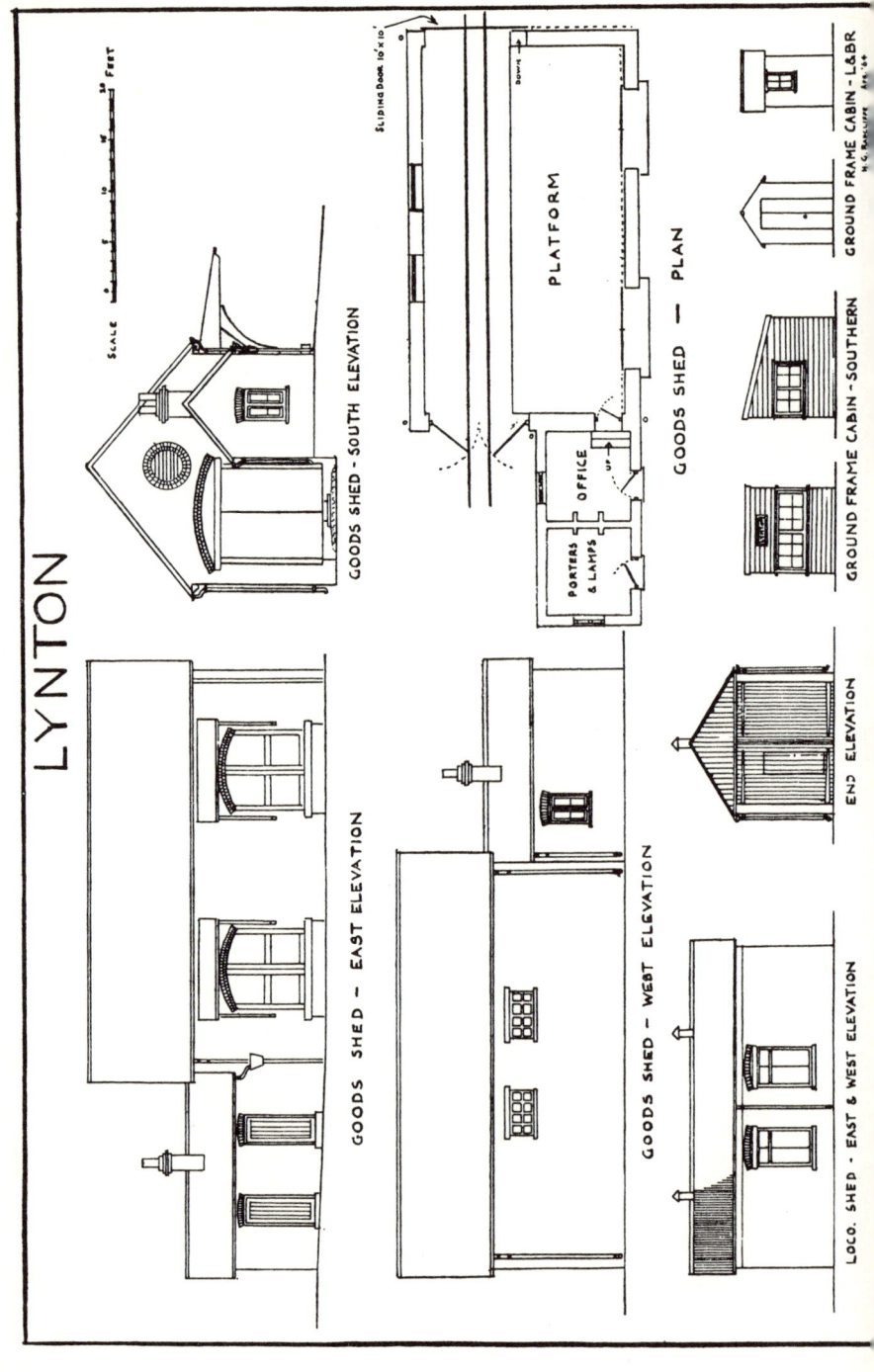

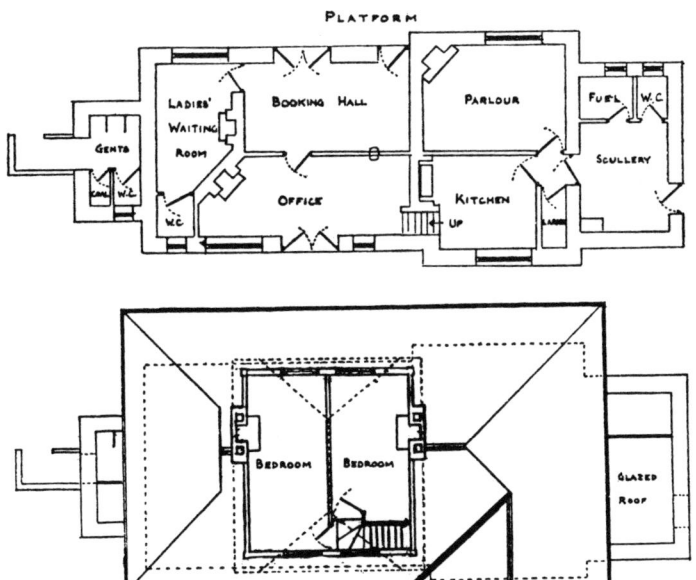
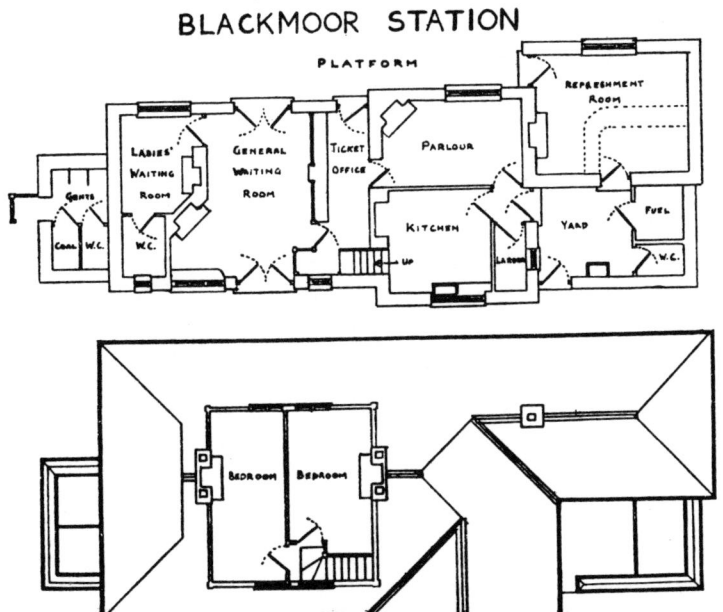

BLACKMOOR STATION

SOUTH ELEVN

NORTH ELEVATION

WEST (PLATFORM) ELEVN

EAST ELEVATION

M G RADCLIFFE APL '64

6: INCOME AND EXPENDITURE 1898-1922

Year	Expenditure	Income	Net Excess of Income over Expenditure	Operating Ratio	Dividend
1898	3,393	4,998	1,605	68	—
1899	5,184	6,418	1,234	81	—
1900	5,861	6,707	846	87	—
1901	5,985	6,810	825	88	—
1902	6,164	7,621	1,457	81	—
1903	6,375	8,071	1,696	79	—
1904	6,464	8,017	1,553	81	—
1905	6,366	8,116	1,750	78	—
1906	6,232	8,892	2,660	70	—
1907	6,669	9,113	2,444	73	—
1908	6,446	9,055	2,609	71	—
1909	6,394	9,396	3,002	68	—
1910	6,859	9,571	2,712	72	—
1911	6,642	9,387	2,745	71	—
1912	6,411	9,228	2,817	69	—
1913	6,640	9,668	3,028	67	½
1914 1915 1916 1917 1918	Not available				
1919	14,490	17,868	3,379	81	½
1920 1921	No useful returns available				
1922	14,948	15,056*	108	99.5	—

* Note that the figure quoted on page 38 is for operating receipts, and does not include miscellaneous receipts for rents, cartage etc, amounting to £545.

7: SOUTHERN NATIONAL OMNIBUS SERVICES BETWEEN BARNSTAPLE AND LYNTON

Mention has been made of the fact that timings of some Southern National Omnibus Services began to appear in the railway timetables from 1931 onwards.

During the 1920s the National Omnibus & Transport Company began to secure a foothold in the West Country and in East Anglia by the acquisition of various local operators. Under 1928 legislation the four main railway companies were permitted to acquire interests in bus companies. One result was that the West Country interests of the National Omnibus & Transport Company were split into the Western National Omnibus Company (operating in Great Western Railway territory and taking over the GW's own bus fleet which had started with two vehicles purchased from the abortive Ilfracombe to Blackmoor Gate service) and the Southern National Omnibus Company (operating in Southern Railway territory).

The Southern Railway steadily increased its holding in the Southern National until in 1931 half of the shares were held. (Eventually the GWR and SR between them held a controlling interest in the three bus companies which provided over 90 per cent of the public road transport in the West Country.)

By the early 1930s the Southern National were operating a service between Barnstaple and Lynton. In spring 1931 this comprised one journey in each direction on Tuesdays and Fridays only, taking 1 hour 38 mins. During the summer of 1931, 1 June until 20 September, the frequency was increased to three journeys each way on weekdays and one on Sundays (increased to three from 5 July).

The first replacement service for the railway in the winter 1935-36 consisted of five Monday to Friday, six Saturday and two Sunday journeys in each direction, which approximated in timings with the train service of the previous year. The running time had by now been reduced to 1 hour 35 mins. For the summer of 1936 there were six Monday to Friday, seven Saturday and four Sunday services each way from 5 July until 27 September.

By comparison, the summer timetable for 1961 offered eight full-length journeys each way taking only 1 hour 11 mins. between Lynton and the Southern National's Barnstaple office (four minutes more to Barnstaple Junction Station), with an extra short trip to Bratton Fleming and back shortly after 6 p.m. The Saturday service was augmented to 11 full-length journeys each way with two short trips to Bratton Fleming. The Sunday service comprised four trips each way. The following winter service comprised seven Monday to Friday, eight Saturday and three Sunday journeys each way throughout with one Monday to Friday and two Saturday 'shorts' to Bratton Fleming. Naturally, this does not present a full picture since duplicate buses were run at relatively short notice.

In the early days the Southern National fleet consisted of a somewhat heterogeneous collection of different makes of vehicles which had been acquired in the process of absorbing various local operators. From the recollections of one of the authors, AEC Reliance vehicles fitted with a mail compartment at the rear were used for several years after the closure of the L & BR. Just before the Second World War the Southern and Western National Companies began to introduce Bristol vehicles and a fairly heavy fleet replacement scheme with vehicles from this manufacturer took place after the war. Both single and double-decker Bristols have been observed on this route in recent years.

As has been mentioned elsewhere, the Minehead—Lynmouth horse-drawn coach service was supplanted by motor buses in 1922, operated by a local concern. This was later taken over by the National Company and is now operated by the Western National.

The area is also served by the Royal Blue express service. There are two routes beyond Yeovil to Ilfracombe: *via* Milverton and Bampton, and *via* Minehead, Lynton, Blackmoor Gate and Combe Martin. In winter there is one service on each route daily; in summer the two daily services are augmented by night journeys to and from London at the weekends.

Acknowledgments and Bibliography

The fact that interest in the Lynton & Barnstaple has been kept alive is in no small measure due to the excellent work *The Lynton & Barnstaple Railway*, first published as an obituary shortly after the line's closure. A pioneer work of its type, it has passed through five editions and been used as a pattern by authors of histories of other narrow-gauge and minor railways. While we have tried to make an entirely new approach, it is inevitable that there will appear certain similarities. We gratefully acknowledge that the late Mr Catchpole has given us a starting point; our own extensive research has, however, been from original sources and had in fact largely been completed before we joined forces to write this book. Background material has come from the books listed at the end of these notes and from the British Transport Historical Records Office and the North Devon Athenæum.

Our thanks are due to the Lynton & Barnstaple Railway Society for their encouragement to produce this more detailed history, and to a host of enthusiasts and local people who have contributed information, or as in the case of the late Mr F. E. Box, left it for us to use. To the men of the Lynton & Barnstaple Railway, now a sadly and steadily diminishing band of whom we should mention among others Messrs A. Nutt, E. Northcombe, the late F. Northcombe, H. Gaydon and H. Stevens, we owe a great debt of gratitude.

Finally, we should particularly like to thank those few who have given us an exceptional amount of help in bringing this book to fruition. To T. M. Trickey (also an old L & BR man), G. A. Tull and H. B. Pritchard for help with detailed material and for checking the manuscript; to R. E. Tustin for assistance and for kindly permitting us to use his drawings of locomotives and rolling stock; and lastly to that railway collector par excellence, W. E. Hayward, who has allowed us free access to his Wehlyn Railway Records in which the Lynton line always takes pride of place.

Since the publication of the first edition valuable additional information on rolling stock has come to hand from Mr D. M. Lee which is incorporated in this edition.

Brown, Gordon A., *The Operation of the Lynton & Barnstaple Railway 1898-1935* (privately published 1960).

Boyd, J. I. C., *The Festiniog Railway*, two volumes (Oakwood Press, 1956 and 1960).
Boyd, J. I. C., *Narrow Gauge Railways in Mid-Wales* (Oakwood Press, 1952).
Burton, S. H., *The North Devon Coast* (Westaway, 1953).
Catchpole, L. T., *The Lynton & Barnstaple Railway* (Oakwood Press, 5th edition, 1963).
W. G. Hoskins, *A New Survey of England: Devon* (Collins, 1954).
Thomas, David St John, *A Regional History of the Railways of Great Britain, Volume One: The West Country* (Phoenix House, second edition, 1963).
The Railway Magazine, The Lynton and Barnstaple Railway: Interview with Sir George Newnes, by Philip Whitwell Wilson, Vol 2, 1898; *The Lynton and Barnstaple Railway*, by J. F. Gairns, Vol 40, 1917; *The Lynton and Barnstaple Railway*, by John W. Dorling, Vol 57, 1935.
The Model Railway Constructor. Articles by R. E. Tustin, 1951 to 1955.

THE ILLUSTRATIONS

N. Devon Athenaeum, plates 1—11, 27, 43, 51, 54; Mr G. A. Tull, plate 12; Lens of Sutton, plates 13, 32, 33, 58; R. L. Knight Limited, plates 15, 19, 23, 36, 40, 41, 55; Mr W. E. Hayward, plate 16; Mr E. Northcombe, plates 17, 45, 48; Mr H. C. Casserley, plates 14, 30, 42, 46, 49, 50, 52, 53, 56; Mr D. E. H. Box, plates 18, 20, 21, 22, 25, 26, 57; Mr H. R. Norman, plates 24, 31; Mr J. D. Prideaux, plates 28, 29, 34, 38, 39, maps and station plans in text; Locomotive & General Railway Photographs, plates 35, 37, 47; Mr H. B. Pritchard, plate 44; Mr J. Lomas, thumb-nail sketches in text; Mr R. E. Tustin, locomotive and rolling stock drawings.

Line drawings of station buildings in text are from drawings by Mr R. J. Sellick, most being based on the original builder's plans kindly made available by Mr. W. H. Jones of Lynton. Frontispiece and ink sketches opposite index and on page 105 by Mr H. G. Radcliffe.

Index

Illustrations are indicated by heavy type

Accidents, 37, 40, 57, 112, **plate 19**
Acetylene lighting, 37, 73, 75
Acts of Parliament: Lynton Railway (1885), 14; L & BR (1895), 15-7, 22, 43; Railway (1921), 39; SR (1923), 38-9, 43
Alexandra, main London train, 88
Anecdotes of the line, 106-8
Animals on the line, 107
Apprentices, 96
Atlantic Coast Express, 88
Auction sales, trains for, 90
Avonside Engine Co., 36, 66, 69
Axle boxes, 27

Bagnall, W. G., 62
Baker, Stationmaster, 32
Baldwin Locomotive Works, Philadelphia, 21, 33, 67, 69, 71
Barbrook, 40, 42, **plate 37**
Barclay, Andrew, 62
Barnstaple, Arms of, **49,** 76
Barnstaple bus service, 41, 112, 124
Barnstaple Castle, 42, 113
Barnstaple Corporation, 31, 76
Barnstaple & District Chamber of Commerce, 42
Barnstaple (GWR), 99, 102
Barnstaple Junction, 99, 102
Barnstaple & Lynton Electric Tramroad Co., 14, 111
Barnstaple Quay station, 16
Barnstaple Town, 16, 17, 18, 23, 30, 31, 45, 46, 48, **50,** 51, 55, 87-8, 90, 96, 97, 98, 103, 105, 106, 115, 116, **plates 11-15**
Barnstaple Yard, 30, 31
Beer, cartage of, 99
Bentley, Mr, 20-1
Bideford, Westward Ho! and Appledore Railway, 35
Bills, various abortive (1879-1892), 14-16; *see also* Acts of Parliament

Blackmoor, 22, 30, 31, 33, 34, 35, 36, 37, 45, 47, 48, 54, 55, 57, **58,** 87, 88, 90, 97, 100, 104, 111, 112, 115, 116, 121, 122, **plates 31-33**
Blackmoor Gate, 14, 17, 18, 27, 37, 41, 48, 90, 124
Board meetings, 17, 21-2, 26-7, 32, 111
Board of Trade Inspection, 21, 22, 33, 112
Board of Trade order for loan, 23
Booking offices, 97-8
Bookstalls, 21, 61
Box, F. E., 30, 109, 126
Boyd, J. I. C., 126
Brakes, hand, 79, 83, **85,** 86; vacuum, 75, 79, 83, 84, **85,** 86, 106
Bran traffic, 102
Bratton Down, 17
Bratton Fleming, 20, 21, 30, 31, 32, 33, 37, 40, 41, 45, 47, 48, 55-7, **58,** 87-8, 90, 94, 97, 100, 103, 104, 112, 115, 116, 124, 125, **plates 27-30**
Bratton Valley, 18, **plates 25 & 26**
Braunton Road level crossing, 37, 40, 51, 53, 87, 96, 112
Braunton Road signal box, 51, 98
Braunton tramway, 111
Bray, Gateman, 31
Brendon, 42
Bricks traffic, 99
Bristol Wagon & Carriage Works Co. Ltd., 23, 73, **74,** 75, 80, 83, **84, 85**
British Transport Historical Records, 126
Brown, Gordon A., 126
Brush Electrical Engineering Co., 63
Burton, S. H., 126

Caffyns Halt, 36, 59, 112, 115, **plate 37**
Carpenter, 96
Carriage cleaner and repairer, 96
Carriage sheds, 53, 115

Carriages, 48; brake, 78; cleaning of, 96, 103; compo-brake, 75-6; observation, 76-8; passenger, 40, 73-9; rolling of, 35; *see also* Rolling stock
Cashmore, John, Ltd., 46
Castle, S., 47
Catchpole, L. T., 126-7
Chains, the, 59
Chambers, Scott & Co., 82, 86
Chanter, C. E. Roberts, 16, 17, 39, 65
Chanter, Francis William, 17, 18-23, 26, 31, 34
Chanter, Rev J. E., 33, 59
Chaplin, Messrs, 99
Chelfham, 18, 21, 30, 31, 32, 34, 35, 37, 45, 47-8, **50,** 54-6, 88, 90, 94, 97, 99, 107, 115, 116, **plates 20-23**
Chelfham viaduct, 19, 54-5, 115, **plates 5 & 6, 20**
Christian, Princess, 108
Chumhill, 55, 112, **plate 24**
Coaches, horse-drawn, 13, 32, 125; motor, 36, 87, 112, 124-5
Coal, prices, 20-1, 35; tenders for supplying, 27, 33-4; traffic, 99, 105; Welsh steam, 99; *see also* Coasters
Coasters, coal, 99, 100, 102, 104-5
Cohen, George & Sons, 40, 82, 86
Cole safety valves, 67
Collar Bridge, 54, **plate 10**
Combe Martin, 13, 14, 59, 111, 125
Confectionery, cartage of, 99
Conference at Barnstaple Castle, 42, 113
Contract, maintenance clause, 28; penalty clause, 23
Countisbury Hill, 13
Cows, traffic in, 101
Cox, E. S., 41, 43
Cranes, 40, 112; breakdown, 86; jib, 47, 116; portable, 46-7; travelling, 82, 107
Crossing sweeper, 96

Dean Steep, 35, 48, **plate 39**
Deer, 18, 56
Devon & Cornish Days, 41
Devon & Somerset Railway, 12, 111
Dewfall, Thomas, 20
Diesel railcars suggested, 42, 109-10
Directors, Founder, 17, 21-2, 26; *see also* Board meetings

Dividend paid, 37-8, 112
Dogs' box, 77-8, 85
Dorling, John W., 118
Double-headed trains, 37, 38, 103-4
Drewett, Charles E., 34, 39, 96, 107, 112
Drivers, anecdote, 107; duties of, 91; employed by L & BR, 20, 21, 30-1, 96; pay of, 32-3; reports, 104
Dykes cottage, 18

Easement for water mains, 36
Eastleigh SR Works, 40, 46, 69
Erridge, F. B:, 16, 29
Evans, O'Connell & Co. Ltd., 21, 26
Excursion trains, 37, 41, 42, 45, 88, 94-5, 103, 109
Exeter & Crediton Railway, 12
Exmoor, transport on, 12-3

Fares, 19, 33
Fennell, H., 33, 104
Festiniog Railway, 15, 38, 48, 63, 65, 78-9, 83, 109, 117
Festiniog Railway, The, 126
Filleigh, 14, 15, 111
Filleigh railway scheme, 15-6
Finance, 11, 22-9, 34, 36, 38, 41, 44, 108-10, 112
Finch & Chanter, 27
Firemen, anecdote, 107; employed by L & BR, 21, 30, 34
First-class travel, 75, 76, 77, 79, 100-1
Flour, 99, 102
Footwarmers, 41, 97
Fortescue, Lord, 15
Fox, Sir Douglas, 33
Fox, Fowler & Co., 16, 26, 29
Fremington, 100
Fursden, R., 20

Gairns, J. F., 118
Gauge, broad, 63; narrow, 11, 14, 15, 16, 42-3, 51, 62, 108-9; standard suggested, 15, 42-3
Gaydon, H., 126
Glover, Fireman, 30
Goodleigh, 54
Goods stock list, 80-1
Gradients, 54, 55, **56,** 57, 61
Grain, 99, 102
Great Western Railway, 12-13, 14, 15,

INDEX 131

22, 33, 36, 42, 99, 102, 124
Groceries, cartage of, 99
Ground frame signal, 51, 99
Guard's compartment, 78, 79; duties, 89, 91
Gull, Sir Cameron, 31

Halliday, W. H., 15, 17, 21
Handbrakes, 79, 83, **85**, 86; pillar-type, 85
Hardware, cartage of, 99
Hart, W. J., 37, 112
Hayward, W. E., 126
Hewitt, Sir Thomas, K.C., 15, 17, 18, 19, 34, 37, 38, 39, 112
Heywood, J., 16
Heywood, W. E., 46
Hides and skins, traffic in, 100
High Bray, 42
Hollerday Hall, 15, 111
Hood, Jacomb, 31
Horse traffic, 12, 13, 17, 99, 100
Hoskins, W. G., 127
Hotels, 12-13, 32, 107
Howard, J. & F., 41, 80, 83, **84, 85,** 86
Hunacott, 18
Hydro-electric plant, 111

Ilfracombe, 13, 36, 45, 51, 87, 112, 124
Inspection trolley, 108, 116, **plate 4**
Iron ore traffic, 100

Jeune, Col E. B., and booking arrangements, 20; chairman (1919), 38, 112; director (1895), 17; and finance of the line, 34; house party, 21; local matters left to, 65; Parracombe site, 19; promotes L & BR, 15
Jeune, Mrs, 15
Jones Bros., 13, 19, 21, 22, 38
Jones, Tom, 100

K & ES Railway, 86
Kentisbury Down, 57
Kerry Tramway, 62

Lancey Brook viaduct, 48, 55, 115, **frontispiece and plate 4**
Lancing Works, 40, 82, 112
Land, cost of, 23, 32
Lartigue monorail system, 14
Level crossing, Braunton Road, 37, 40, 51, 53, 87, 96, 112
Light engines, 91, 92
Lighting, acetylene, 37, 73, 75; oil, 37, 73
Lime, cartage of, 16
Litigation, L & BR v Nuttall, 22, 27-9, 33, 34, 112
Litson, William, 12
Livery, of carriages, 76-7; of goods wagons, 79; of locomotives, 66, 67, 69, 71, 72
Livestock, cartage of, 100-1
Locomotives, repairs, 65-6
Locomotive sheds, 53, 61, 115
Locomotives, Baldwin, 66-7, **68,** 69, 71; choice of, 19; comparative dimensions of, 72; diesel suggested, 42, 109-10; *Excelsior*, 62, **plate 1;** *Exe*, 43, 46-7, **64,** 65, **70,** 71, 72, 114, **frontispiece and plates 13 & 46;** *Kilmarnock*, 34, 62-3, 83, **plate 5;** *Lew*, 40, 45, 46-7, 69, **70,** 71, 72, 112, 113, 114, **plates 29 & 47;** livery, 66, 67, 69, 71, 72; *Lyn*, 33, 36, 46-7, 66-7, 66, **68,** 69, 71, 106-7, 112, 113, **plates 14, 16, 32, 48-50;** Manning Wardle & Co., 20, 23, 40, 46, 63-7, 69-71, 111, **plates 45-47;** nameplates of, 46; pilot, 104; *Slave*, 62, **plates 3 & 45;** *Spondon*, 63; standby, 108; *Taw*, 21, 46-7, 65-6, **70,** 71, 72, 111, 114, **plates 22, 36 & 57;** *Winnie*, 62-3; *Yeo*, 21, 31, 45, 46-8, 65, **70,** 71, 111, 114, **plates 7, 33, 42, 45 & 50**
Locomotives, types of, 62, 65-6, 67, 71-2
Lodge, Driver ,30, 31
Lodging-out turns, 90, 96
London & South Western Railway, 12-4, 18, 22, 23, 31, 34, 36, 61, 96, 98, 111, 112
Lynmouth, 12-13, 35
Lynton, bus service, 124; growth of, 16; goods yard, 61, 86; signal cabin, 116; station, 18, 20, 30, 31, **32, 35,** 38, 40, 45, 47, 61, 87, 88, **97, 106,** 115, **118, 119, 129, plates 7, 40-44**
Lynton & Barnstaple Railway, anecdotes of, 106-8; Bill (1883), 111; (1885), 14, 111; (1895), 15-7, **22, 43;** board of, 17, 33, 34, 73; closure of,

42-4, 45-9, 108, **plate 23**; construction of, 17-29; and SR, 30, 38, 39-44, 90, 108, 112; delay in construction, 18, 27; crest, **49**; directors, 17, 21-2, 26, 73; early years of, 32-4; equipment, 97-9; first proposals for, 14-6, 111; first through train, **plate 43**; goods stock list, 80-1; income and expenditure, 123; last train, 45, 110, 113; livery, 66, 67, 69, 71, 72, 76-7, 79; London connection, 42, 88; opening of, 11, 20-1, 30-2, 111, 112, **plate 17**; open to general traffic, 32, 112; operation of, 87-96; permanent way, condition of, 109; profit on, 110; prospectus, 17; route, the, 51-61; sale of, 46-8, 78, 86, 113, 116; staff, 20, 21, 30-5, 91, 96-7, 99, 104, 107-8, 110; tickets, 101, 112, **plate 58**; timetables, 20, 34, 35, 41, 87-96, 105, 112; track, cost of renewal, 108-9; usage of, 11

Lynton & Barnstaple Railway, The, 126

Lynton & Barnstaple Railway Society 126

Lynton & Lynmouth Cliff Funicular Railway, 15, 111

Lynton Urban District Council, 42, 43, 45, 82

Lynton Water Co., 19, 35

McDougall, Mr, 20
Mail, 88, 103, 107, 109-10
Manning Wardle & Co., 20, 23, 40, 46, 63-7, 69-71, 111, **plates 45-47**
Manure, cartage of, 99, 102
Market day traffic, 88, 89, 90, 91, 94, 101-2, 110
Martinhoe Common, 59
Martinhoe Cross, 17, 19
Martinhoe Cutting, 63
Masters, Signalman, 31
Mellor, Smith & May, 27
Milne, Driver, 30
Minehead, 42, 125
Minehead—Lynmouth Light Railway scheme, 32, 33, 112
Minerals, cartage of, 100, 102
Mintern, Mr, 56
Minute book, the company's, 22, 100
Model Railway Constructor, The, 127

Motor coach feeder service, 36
Motor coach service, 87, 112, 124-5
Motor transport, competition from, 36-7, 41-2, 101-2, 108, 124
Mountain, Sir Edward, 39

Narrow Gauge Railways in Mid-Wales, 126
National Provincial Bank, Barnstaple, 29
New Survey of England, A, 127
Newnes, Lady, 15, 17, 21, 31-2, 111
Newnes, Sir Frank, 31, 39
Newnes, Sir George, article on, 118; appointed chairman of L & BR, 17; death of, 37; experiments with motor coach service, 36; Hollerday Hall built for, 15, 111; life of, 15; and L & SWR deadlock, 18; and Minehead & Lynmouth Light Railway, 33; opening ceremony, 21, 31-2, 35; opinion on *Lyn,* 69; his prize for best kept station, 56; promotes L & BR, 15-6; report at board meeting (1897), 23
Newspapers, 88, 103
Northcombe, E., 126
Northcombe, F., 33, 126
North Devon Athenaeum, 126
North Devon Coast, The, 126
North Devon Herald, 28, 33
North Devon Journal, 32
North Devon Railway, 12, 111
Norton Fitzwarren, 13
Norwegian couplings, 75
Nutt, A., 126
Nuttall, James, contractor for L & BR, 19, 20, 59; financial difficulties of, 28; litigation, 22, 27-9, 33-4, 112; tender for L & BR, 22, 26, 111
Nuttall, James Jnr., 19-20, 22, 27, 111

Observation coaches, 76-8
Offals, cartage of, 102
Oil lighting, 37, 73
Omnibuses, hotel, 32
Opening of the line, 11, 20-1, 30-2, 111, 112, **plate 17**
Operation of the Lynton & Barnstaple Railway, 1898-1936, The, 126

Packhorses, 12

INDEX

Painters, 96
Paper train, 88, 103
Parcels traffic, 99, 109, 110
Parracombe embankment, 48, 57, 63
Parracombe Halt, 17, 19, 33, 34, 45, 55, 56-7, 56, 59, 91, 106, 112, 115, 116, **plates 34 & 35**
Passenger traffic, excursionists, 37, 41, 42, 45, 88, 103, 109; market day, 88-91, 101-2, 110; service criticized, 94, 96; statistics of, 100-1, 112
Passing loop at Bratton Fleming, 94, 98, 103
Pearce, Foreman Fitter, 31
Permanent way, 39-40, 42
Permanent Way Inspector, 20, 96
Peto, Sir Basil, M.P., 43
Pickfords, Messrs., 99
Pilkington, R., 20, 21, 30
Pilot engine, 104
Pilton Bridge signal box, 31, 54, 97, 98
Pilton office, 107-8
Pilton Wharf, 39, 115
Pilton Yard, 35, **52,** 53, 89, 94; carriages built at, 75; closing, 45-6; coal wagons loaded at, 104-5; demolition of trains at, 47; dimension of, 115-6; in early years, 87; goods brake van built at, 112; goods loaded at, 90, 103; *Lyn* assembled at, 67; market day working, 37; opening of line, 21, 30-1; repair shops, 43, 83, 86; sheds at, 99; signals at, 98; staff at, 96; today, 48
Pitprops, traffic in, 100
Platelayers, 96, 97, 112
Platforms, metalling of, 20; length of, 115
Points, operation of, 51-2, 53, 54, 61, 98
Porlock Hill, 13
Porter, E., 100
Porters, 97
Porter-signalman, 97
Portland stone tramways, 62
Potatoes, cartage of, 100, 102
Powell Group, 35
Press, the, 21, 111, **plate 9**
Pritchard, H. B., 126
Publicity, 41
Rabbits, cartage of, 100

Railway Magazine, The, 127
Ramsbottom safety valves, 69
Refreshment rooms, 19
Richards, Smith, 22
Rolle Quay, 11, 51, 53, **plates 1 & 57**
Rolling stock, acquisition of, 112: bogie goods wagons, 46-7, 79; bogie wagon, 8-ton open, 37, 40, 112; brake van, 8-ton covered, 37, 41, 85, 99, 102, 104, 112; coaches, 26, 27; coal trucks, 35; compo-brake coaches, 36, 75, 103; freight, **plates 54-56;** goods brake vans, 85; goods stock, 79-86; inspection trolley, 108, 116, **plate 4;** jib-cranes, 47, 116; match truck, 40, 82, 112; observation carriages, 76-8; open wagons, 4-wheeled, 47; passenger carriages, 40-8, 73-9, **plates 51-53;** platform wagons, 36; repairs, 40; service vehicles, 82; trucks, open, 46
Romney, Hythe & Dymchurch Railway, 47
Rowley Cross, 57
Royal Blue express coach service, 125

Salter safety valves, 62, 65
Sanders & Co., 21
Sanders & Ridges, 27
Service vehicles, 82
Shambleway, 17
Shapland & Petter, **74,** 75
Shares, 23, 27, 38
Sheep, traffic in, 101
Sheer legs, 53
Shunting spur, 53
Sidings, 53, 55, 56, 57, 61, 99, 115
Signal and Telegraph Linesman, 96
Signal boxes, 31, 47, 51, 53, 54, 98, 116
Signalling apparatus, 21, 23, 26, 98
Signalmen, 31, 96, 99
Signal posts, 40
Signals, double arm, 53
Smith, W. H. & Son, 21
Snapper Halt, 35, 47-8, 54, 78, 91, 94, 107, 112, 115, **plate 19**
Snow blocks line, 35
Soap, cartage of, 99
Southern National Omnibus Service, 41, 94, 112, 124-5
Southern Railway, 42, 43, 124; ab-

sorbs L & BR, 30, 38, 39-44, 90, 108, 112; alteration to carriages, 76; alterations to station buildings, 38; close line, 110; decreasing traffic, 83; goods working, 98; improvements to line, 96; lifts track, 113; livery, 71, 79; purchases breakdown cranes, 86; should operate summer service only, 109; traffic statistics, 102
Southern Railway Act (1923), 39, 112
South Molton, 14, 111
Sowden, Henry, 35
Spooner, Mr, 15
Staff, 20-1, 30-5, 91, 96-7, 99, 104, 107-8, 110
Stationmasters, 20, 32, 35, 97, 107-8
Stations, drawings of, **117-122;** Woody Bay (Wooda Bay), **29, 121**
Steam heating equipment, 41, 69, 71, 77, 78, 79, 97, 103, 112
Stephenson inside valve gear, 71
Stevens, H., 126
Stoke Rivers, 55
Summer schedule, 94, 99, 102
Summer service only suggested, 109
Sunday service, 41, 94-5, 97, 105
Sunday service, motor coach, 124-5
Swimbridge, 42
Szlumper, Sir James, 16, 18, 19, 20, 26, 27

Talyllyn Railway, 109
Telegraph apparatus, 21, 23, 26, 99
Third-class travel, 75, 76, 77, 78, 79, 100-1
Tickets issued, 101, 112, **plate 58**
Timber, cartage of, 99
Timetables, 20, 34, 35, 41, 87-96, 105, 112, 124
Track, cost of, 108-9; description of, 97; removal of, 113
Traffic, affected by motor car and lorry, 101-2; coal, 99, 105; day trippers, 37, 88, 101; fall in, 41-2, 83; goods, 99-102, 108, 109; goods, general, 102, 103; goods statistics, 100-2; goods, small, 110; summer, 43, 101, 109; horses, 99; livestock, 100-1; mail, 109, 110; market day, 88, 89, 90, 91, 94, 101-2, 110; minerals, 100, 102; passenger, 33, 37, 41-2, 45, 88, 100-1, 103, 109, 110; pattern of, 100-2; slate, 56; timber, 99
Trains, double-headed, 37, 38, 103-4; Sunday, 41, 94-5, 97, 105
Trickey, T. M., 126
Tull, G. A., 126
Turntables, 19, 47, 53, 73, 115, **plate 56**
Tustin, R. E., 126, 127
Tyer's automatic table, 97

Urie, Mr, 69

Vacuum brakes, 75, 79, 83, 84, 85, 86, 106
Vale of Rheidol Railway, 62, 109
Vallance, Mr, 31
Valley of Rocks Hotel, 32
Valve gear, inside, 71; Joy's, 65, 71; outside, 62; Stephenson, 71
Valves, Cole safety, 67; Ramsbottom safety, 69; Salter safety, 62, 65
Vans, bogie, 46-7; brake, 37, 41, 85, 99, 102, 104, 112
Vegetables, cartage of, 102
Victoria, Princess, 108

Walker, Sir Herbert, 43
Water column, 51, 53, 57
Water-gauge glasses, 106-7
Water supply, 18, 19, 20, 30, 34, 35
Water tanks, 55, 59
Weighbridge, 47, 53, 116
Western National Omnibus Co., 124
Westlandpound, 57
Willis, W. T., 21, 30, 33
Wilson, Philip Whitwell, 118
Winter schedule, 88, 90, 91, 94
Woody Bay (Wooda Bay), hotel, 107; station, 17, **29,** 30, 31, 33, 35, 36, 37, 40, 43, 45, 47, 59, **60,** 88, 90, 94, 97, 100, 106, 107, 112, 115, 116, **121, plates 3, 9, 36 & 47**
Wool traffic, 100
World War I, 37-8, 90, 100, 102; II, 110, 125
Wreath for 'dead' railway, 45

Yeo River, 17
Yeotown, 54
Yorke, Col, 21
York Railway Museum, 46
Youlston Wood, 55